The Acceptance of Human Resource Innovation

LESSONS
FOR
MANAGEMENT

Ellen Ernst Kossek

Foreword by Victor H. Vroom

QUORUM BOOKS
New York • Westport, Connecticut • London

Library of Congress Cataloging-in-Publication Data

Kossek, Ellen Ernst.
    The acceptance of human resource innovation.

    Bibliography: p.
    Includes index.
    1. Personnel management.   I. Title.
HF5549.5.C6K67   1989   658.3   88–32143
ISBN 0–89930–374–9 (lib. bdg. : alk. paper)

British Library Cataloguing in Publication Data is available.

Library of Congress Catalog Card Number: 88–32143
ISBN: 0–89930–374–9

First published in 1989 by Quorum Books

Greenwood Press, Inc.
88 Post Road West, Westport, Connecticut 06881

Printed in the United States of America

∞

The paper used in this book complies with the
Permanent Paper Standard issued by the National
Information Standards Organization (Z39.48–1984).

10 9 8 7 6 5 4 3 2 1

THE ACCEPTANCE OF
HUMAN RESOURCE
INNOVATION

Recent Titles from Quorum Books

Contents

Illustrations

Foreword

The evidence is mounting that the modern corporation is experiencing unprecedented demands for change. Global competition, deregulation, and the changing demographic composition of the labor force are but a few of the external forces that create a turbulent environment for today's managers. As Tichy and Devanna have pointed out in their book, *The Transformational Leader*, maintaining the status quo is no longer a viable option. American companies need to make fundamental, revolutionary changes in order to stay competitive.

Human resource practices and policies are among the areas most frequently cited as needing change. Scholars and practitioners alike stress that if we are to compete effectively with Japan, we must do a better job motivating employees. Similarly, the increasing number of women in the labor force challenges us to look creatively at the interdependence of work and family and to design human resource policies so that the two social systems can complement one another. In addition, the elimination of laws protecting firms from the competitive forces in the market place emphasizes the need for organizational structures that are conducive to initiative, creativity, and entrepreneurship within the corporation.

Thus, human resource policies are being elevated to center stage in the struggle for survival. What used to be one of the least significant management functions—so much so that the personnel or human resource department has frequently become the dumping ground for managers that have not made the grade in marketing, manufacturing, or finance—is emerging in the minds of many as a critical ingredient in the struggle for corporate survival. It goes without saying that current conditions require a level of talent and inventiveness that has not previously been characteristic of human resource management.

In our current environment, innovation in the way in which we manage our human resources is as important as innovation in products and services or in the ways in which these products and services are produced and marketed. The search for better ways of doing things must typify all aspects of the enterprise.

A critical ingredient in that search process must be a means of evaluating the effectiveness of innovations. We should value change not for its own sake but rather embrace selectively those innovations that can be demonstrated to "work better." Organizational learning, like individual learning, requires that we receive feedback concerning the consequence of actions and reinforce those policies and programs that have demonstrated utility in the attainment of our goals.

In a recent book, *The New Leadership*, Arthur Jago and I have distinguished two components of the effectiveness of organizational decisions. Decisions, including those that can be termed innovations, can be evaluated in terms of their quality and their acceptance. I use the term quality in the same sense as the late Professor Norman Maier of the University of Michigan: to refer to the technical aspects of the decision—the degree to which it is consistent with the goals that one seeks to attain and with potentially available information about its consequences. Thus, a high-quality innovation is one which is well "thought through." The second component is the acceptance or commitment to the innovation on the part of those organizational members who have to use it or administer it.

These two components work hand-in-hand. To ask which is more important is like asking which is the more important in determining the area of a rectangle—its height or its width. The importance of each is dependent on the preexisting value of the other. It makes no sense to have a brilliantly conceived innovation which is resisted and opposed by those who are affected by it; nor does it make any sense to have great acceptance of a changed course that is inherently unsound and ill conceived.

In this book Professor Ellen Ernst Kossek describes a pioneering investigation into the acceptance of human resource innovation. Working within a large insurance company, she employed survey research methodology to assess the degree of employee acceptance of eight human resource innovations ranging in character from quality circles to flextime. Her study goes beyond a simple evaluation of these programs by discussing the sources of their differential effectiveness and examining the kinds of employees who are likely to be more or less supportive of each.

For the human resource manager, there are valuable lessons to be gleaned from these pages about how human resource innovations should be designed and introduced. For researchers, whether in academe or in the corporate world, the study breaks new ground in developing a measure of employee acceptance of innovation and a methodology that can and should be used in future investigations of the effectiveness of human resource innovation.

Victor H. Vroom
John G. Searle Professor of
Organization and Management
Yale University
New Haven, Connecticut

Preface

It is my hope that this book will be useful to a wide range of readers, from managers of human resource innovations and personnel researchers to any organizational member who has ever desired greater effectiveness in the administration of new personnel programs. The examination of the history of adoption of eight human resource management innovations at the Valiant Insurance Corporation and the varying level of organizational acceptance to these programs should be of particular interest to managers and academicians who are interested in understanding the nature of the human resource management innovation process. The finding that executives and managers accept innovations more than lower level employees, particularly those innovations designed for nonmanagers, will hopefully encourage future efforts aimed at designing work innovations that better reflect the needs and interests of employees.

The author's decision to study acceptance of new personnel practices can be attributed mainly to reflection upon previous working life experiences as a human resource professional at several companies that are renowned for their management of employees. It is believed that the gap between the stated purpose of a new human resource management (HRM) program in design and its achievement in actuality is generally much larger than desirable. The purpose of this book is to make initial headway toward understanding the "HRM gap."

I would like to express my appreciation to the people who have contributed to this book. This study owes its existence to the cooperation and financial support of my client organization. In particular, I am grateful to the employees who chose to participate in the research and contribute to my knowledge about human resource management innovation by sharing their time and thoughts. In addition, I am grateful to the faculty at the Yale School of Organization and Management who comprised my dissertation committee and aided me in the implementation of this study by providing thoughtful guidance and advice. Victor Vroom, the chairman of the committee, Clayton Alderfer and Rosabeth Moss Kanter all provided valuable commentary on my work. Liliane Miller, the acquisitions editor at Quorum, was also a pleasure to work with on the manuscript. Lastly, and most importantly, the members of my family, my husband, Sandy, and two children, Andrew and newborn Sarah, deserve considerable thanks for their patience and support during my completion of this project.

1

Human Resource Innovation

...the consequences of innovation have generally been understudied...
Much past research has asked: "What variables are related to innovativeness?" While such inquiry has played a useful role in the past, future
investigations need to ask: "What are the *effects* [emphasis added] of adopting innovations?"

Everett Rogers
Diffusion of Innovations
New York: Free Press, 1983

Everett Rogers, a well-known scholar of organizational innovations, identified a
major problem often associated with the adoption of human resource management
(HRM) innovations by employers. Although innovative personnel programs are
frequently adopted to improve the workplace, many organizations fail to systematically evaluate their effectiveness after implementation. The personnel arena
has often been plagued by fads, ranging from T-groups in the 1960s to quality
circles in the 1970s to personnel practices designed to create entrepreneurial
corporate cultures in the 1980s. Unfortunately, academic research has rarely
been used by practitioners for program development and improvement.[1] Also,
despite the fact that HRM innovations are typically introduced to achieve such

worthy goals as improving productivity and employee morale, they generally fall short of management expectations.[2]

The failed promise of many new personnel programs cannot only be attributed to an overemphasis on invention over systematic implementation and evaluation, but also to the rationale spurring their adoption. A variety of reasons can be given for organizational innovation involving the management of human resources. Personnel departments and many HRM policies were first developed in the United States during World War I and the Great Depression as a reaction to these periods of tight labor market conditions and increased union activity.[3] Historically, experimentation with bureaucratic methods has also been done to make labor control appear more ''natural'' and in workers' interests.[4] The more enlightened management of the 1980s may adopt new work practices to foster member commitment and improve the quality of work life (QWL) as well.[5] However, organizations prone to faddishness may initiate HRM innovations to appear more legitimate in their environments.[6] The prime impetus for the introduction of a personnel practice may be because competitors have already done so, or because the practice is the latest panacea being touted by the local management consulting group. Regardless of the rationale behind adoption, however, it is clear, as A. P. Chandler first noted in his classic, *Strategy and Structure*, that organizational innovation is an inextricable part of the American industrial experience in the twentieth century.[7]

RATIONALE FOR STUDY OF ACCEPTANCE OF HRM INNOVATION

There is still much to be understood about when organizational innovations in human resource management successfully take hold and when they do not. Although changes in structure to follow strategy have been thoughtfully studied by researchers such as Chandler, those involving personnel practices have received less attention as innovations. The problems of adopting and sustaining progressive work practices have important societal significance, and this book attempts to make initial headway toward understanding the conditions fostering successful HRM initiatives.

A key problem inhibiting assessment of human resource management innovations stems from the difficulties that often arise in measuring their impact. If a company adopts a new profit-sharing program, for example, it may be days, weeks, months, or even years before the question of effectiveness can be addressed. And it may never be addressed. Perhaps an economic recession affects the firm's key product markets, and there are no profits for a few years. The profit-sharing program may have been very well designed, but the question of its effectiveness cannot be answered. In addition, responses to questions of effectiveness will differ greatly between organizational members. It is likely that an hourly employee's assessment of effectiveness will differ from that of a senior vice president, for example. A much easier, but nonetheless worthwhile, question to answer than the one of effectiveness is raised in this book: "When are human resource management innovations accepted?" A key assumption here is that acceptance of HRM innovation is a necessary but insufficient condition for effectiveness.

This book views new human resource management programs as organizational innovations and examines the relationship between employee characteristics (e.g., hierarchical level, race, sex, and seniority) and behaviors, and acceptance of HRM innovation. Survey data on attitudes toward and use of a sample of personnel innovations were collected from several thousand employees at a major Fortune company. The innovations studied include quality circles, flextime, flexible benefits, job posting, cash awards, a fitness program, a peer recognition award, and an employee-run newsletter. The results are shared with the reader to give insight into the differential impact of implementing HRM innovations on employees and organizational units. To this end, the study also considers the congruence between the expectations and assumptions behind the adoption of the HRM innovations and employee responses to them.

PLAN OF BOOK

Definitions of human resource management innovation and acceptance of innovation, and an interdisciplinary review of theory from the innovation, personnel, and organizational development literatures are found in the latter sections of this chapter. Chapter 2 describes the research design, the organization, and the innovations included in the study. Critical historical events in the adoption of the innovations are described in chapter 3. Chapter 4 contains the measures used in the HRM innovation survey and provides major highlights of the survey results. Chapter 5 discusses findings from statistical analyses of significant differences in acceptance of HRM innovation as a function of various employee backgrounds, unit differences, and the properties of the innovations themselves. Chapter 6 includes a discussion of strategic lessons in the management of HRM innovations for research and practice. Conclusions and an examination of methodological issues are found in chapter 7.

HRM INNOVATION DEFINED

Although companies frequently adopt new ways of managing their employees, it is not always apparent which of these changes are innovations and which are not. This confusion partially can be attributed to the lack of agreement on a definition of an organizational innovation.[8] One major school of thought defines an innovation as the first or very early use of an idea by an organization.[9] The other main school views an innovation as the first use of an idea *within* a firm regardless of whether it has been tried elsewhere.[10] This research uses the latter, more common definition and applies it to the area of human resource management.

A *human resource management innovation*, a type of organizational innovation, is any program, policy, or practice designed to influence employee attitudes and behaviors that is perceived to be new by members.[11] This definition distinguishes organizational innovation from organizational change. As Gerald Zaltman, Robert Duncan and Johnny Holbek observe, "All innovations imply change. Not all change involves innovation, since not everything an organization adopts is perceived as new."[12] An innovation is the change object, whereas organizational change is the alteration of the social system.[13] The magnitude of change that occurs is dependent on the extent to which the innovation receives organizational acceptance. Using a marketing analogy, an innovation is a new product, and the level of acceptance is reflected by the degree to which the market responds favorably to the product.

ACCEPTANCE OF HRM INNOVATION FRAMEWORK

Acceptance of HRM innovation is the extent to which individuals, groups, and the organization adopt social processes that are supportive of the innovation. Attitudinal acceptance is measured through the possession of favorable reactions to the innovation. An employee decision to use an innovation that is optional, such as enrolling in a flexible benefits plan or volunteering to join a quality circle group, can be viewed as accepting behavior.

Acceptance of innovation can be seen as a form of organizational change and can occur at varying levels. That is, few innovations are completely rejected or completely accepted, with the majority found somewhere in the middle range. The framework of organizational acceptance shown in figure 1.1 has four levels: awareness, attitudinal, behavioral, and institutional. For illustrative purposes, the framework is first presented at the individual level of analysis.

Initially, an organizational member becomes *aware* of the personnel innovation and familiar with its features and goals. At the second level of acceptance, a member develops *attitudes* toward the innovation. Attitudes toward an innovation are largely influenced by the extent to which an individual believes that the innovation's features are congruent with personal needs. A working parent with two children under five years of age will probably consider the newly opened company day care center to be highly relevant to his or her working needs. Regardless of the favorability of the individual's assessment of the quality of the way the innovation is administered or whether he or she intends to use the center, the individual will have developed strong attitudes toward the innovation. In contrast, if an employee is aware of an innovation, but doesn't perceive it to be personally relevant, indifference may develop. A 60-year-old employee will probably consider a new day care program to be of little personal consequence. The individual will be indifferent toward the program or may even have negative attitudes toward the innovation if he or she perceives pension resources are being diverted to support the center.

At the third level, a member alters *behavior* to support the attitude change.

Figure 1.1
Levels of Acceptance

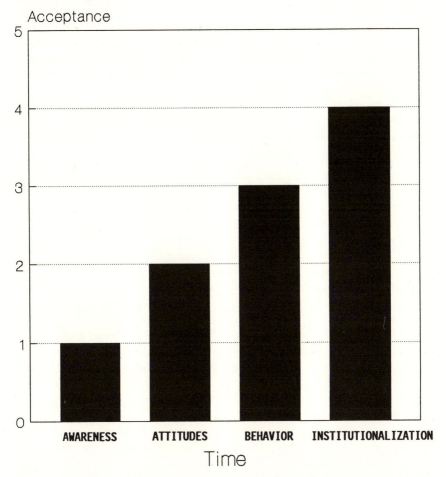

Even if a member does hold favorable attitudes toward the innovation, changing behavior sometimes can be difficult due to organizational constraints. Sometimes individuals may possess a positive orientation toward an innovation but do not use it because of its nonavailability or its incongruence with their situation.[14] For example, a top manager may have a very positive orientation toward quality circles, but may be unable to participate directly in the circles because they are designed for subordinates. Despite the fact that the manager may personally believe that the principles of quality circles could be applied to senior employees, the manager is unable to demonstrate acceptance through participation because of inhibitory organizational norms.

The highest level of acceptance is *institutionalization* of the innovation. At this level, a member incorporates behaviors supporting the initiative into his or her work repertoire over a sustained period of time. It should be observed that many HRM innovations fail to be institutionalized.

Although it is easiest to present the model sequentially, the stages are non-discrete. Movement up to higher levels may first entail regression to an earlier stage. For example, sometimes in order for behavioral acceptance to occur, regression to the attitudinal stage may be required as attitudes are refined in response to the increasing amount of information acquired on the innovation.

LEVELS OF ACCEPTANCE

Acceptance of innovation can be measured for individuals, groups, and organizations. An individual employee's attitude toward and use of an innovation can be easily measured. Acceptance of innovation also can be differentiated by the general attitudes and behaviors of certain groups of employees. Perhaps executives love quality circles, whereas union members view them as another management scheme to get employees to work harder for no additional pay. Or maybe only female employees opt to take parental child care leave, despite the innovation's availability to male employees as well.

Moving to the organizational level of analysis, acceptance can be indicated in a variety of ways. The voluntary *diffusion* or migration of an innovation from one unit to another can indicate acceptance and provides evidence of organizational learning. The provision of *sustained financial and social support* from organizational leaders and groups also shows acceptance at the organizational level. *Permeation* of an innovation into the work environment, the extent that it is viewed less as a separate program and more as an integral part of the employee-organization relationship, is another sign of acceptance. For example, whereas quality circles in one company are viewed as a program that is quite separate from workers' daily routine, their introduction in another firm may have infused a participative culture and way of thinking throughout the entire organization. Clearly, the innovation has permeated the work environment to a much greater degree in the latter case. Lastly, the publicizing of an innovation to such external groups as stockholders, the local community, and other organizations also evinces acceptance at the organizational level.

PREVIOUS RESEARCH ON HRM INNOVATION

There is very little academic research specifically focused on the subject of HRM innovation. In order to provide a context for the current study, it is necessary to use an interdisciplinary approach integrating findings from the innovation, personnel/HRM, and organizational development (OD) and change fields, which are discussed below.

INNOVATION RESEARCH

Innovation research has generally been targeted on the study of technological innovations over administrative ones, and has concentrated primarily on issues of adoption and diffusion. Whereas adoption scholars focus on "understanding what makes an organization responsive to its environment," diffusion scholars seek to understand "why and how an innovation—or group of innovations—spreads in a population."[15] Consequently, the field has given insufficient attention to the study of managerial or administrative innovations and issues of implementation. There has often been little concern with the quality of adoption and the differential impact of adoption on organizational members or with the effect of the properties of innovations on acceptance. Despite these problems, application of concepts from the innovation field is extremely helpful in providing a framework for understanding HRM innovations.

Adoption of Innovation

Differences between innovation-adopting and nonadopting organizations or early and late adopters have been attributed to a large list of often inconclusive factors. As Downs and Mohr observe, "Perhaps the most alarming characteristic of the body of empirical study of innovation has been the extreme variation among its findings. . . . Factors found to be important in one study are found to be considerably less important, not important at all, or even inversely important in another study. This phenomenon occurs with relentless regularity."[16]

Actually, the state of the adoption field is not quite as dismal as painted, if these factors are viewed as being positively related to the initial adoption of innovation. Organizations that have organic structures[17] or adopt temporary ones such as parallel structures,[18] that are comprised of members with elite values,[19] that are at or near the top of their interorganizational prestige hierarchies,[20] and are in dynamic environments[21] tend to initiate a high number of innovations.

Although disagreeing over the names and number of stages, adoption researchers generally view innovation as a process with discrete steps. Table 1.1 shows Everett Rogers' classical model; it includes two main stages, initiation and implementation, which each have several substages.[22] The model provides a good framework for understanding the innovation process, particularly if one takes the view that these stages are not discrete and sometimes overlap. Rogers' model is used to analyze the adoption of HRM innovations in chapter 3.

HRM Innovation Properties

Innovation research on adoption has generally distinguished between technical and administrative innovations. One popular "dual-core" model by R. L. Daft, for example, proposes that technical and administrative innovations are initiated in different structures for different reasons. Technical innovations are fostered

Table 1.1

Rogers' Model of Stages of the Innovation Process in Organizations

Stage in the Innovation Process	Major Activities at Each Stage in the Innovation Process
I. Initiation:	All of the information-gathering, conceptualizing, and planning for the adoption of an innovation, leading up to the decision to adopt.
1. Agenda-setting	General organizational problems, which may create a perceived need for an innovation, are defined; the environment searched for innovations of potential value to the organization.
2. Matching	A problem from the organization's agenda is considered together with an innovation, and the fit between them is planned and designed.
--------------------------The Decision to Adopt--------------------------	
II. Implementation:	All of the events, actions, and decisions involved in putting an innovation into use.
3. Redefining/Restructuring	(1) The innovation is modified and re-invented to fit the situation of the particular organization and its perceived problem, and (2) organizational structures directly relevant to the innovation are altered to accommodate the innovation.
4. Clarifying	The relationship between the innovation and the organization is defined more clearly as the innovation is put into full and regular use.
5. Routinizing	The innovation eventually loses its separate identity and becomes an element in the organization's ongoing activities.

Reprinted with permission of The Free Press, a Division of Macmillan, Inc. from *Diffusion of Innovations*, Third Edition, by Everett M. Rogers. Copyright © 1962, 1971, 1983 by The Free Press.

in organic structures due to environmental uncertainty, whereas administrative innovations such as HRM initiatives are fostered in mechanistic structures due to internal needs for coordination and direction.[23]

Although such a dichotomy is useful because it highlights the relationship between organizational structure and innovation, it seems incomplete in its application to HRM innovation. Many human resource innovations ranging from day care assistance to quality circles are not necessarily adopted due to needs for coordination and direction, but are more conceivably adopted because of environmental uncertainty stemming from a respective increase in dual career couples and a rise in imported goods. Or perhaps neither of these rational explanations are appropriate. Maybe these innovations were adopted because the top executive heard that they were implemented at another organization by a top officer he or she admires and would like to imitate.

By studying a sample of HRM innovations adopted at a firm, the current study explores the relationship between acceptance and the properties of the HRM programs. It is believed that some HRM innovations have a more central impact on the quality of employee working life than others. For example, innovations such as flextime or a piece rate pay system affect an employee's on-the-job working environment and are likely to directly influence a supervisor's day-to-day management of subordinates. Other innovations such as a day care referral service and cafeteria benefits, although important advances, are essentially removed from an employee's daily working environment and have minimal impact on supervisory responsibilities. This assumption that acceptance may vary according to the characteristics of the HRM innovations will provide a foundation for analysis of differences in acceptance of different types of HRM innovations, found at the end of chapter 5.

Implementation of Innovation

It is striking to note that a major review of 1500 studies of innovations found that less than 3% dealt with the consequences of innovations.[24] There are several key reasons for this lack of interest. Most research tends to be sponsored by change agencies that tacitly assume the innovation's consequences will be positive. In addition, most studies are cross-sectional, involving large mailings of surveys where the researchers had no personal contact with the firms. Also, consequences are difficult to measure, because their assessment is subjective and value-laden and are often confounded with other effects.

Despite these difficulties, a small number of implementation studies have been conducted that merit brief review, particularly because all of them except one examined personnel innovations. W. R. Nord and S. Tucker's rich case study of the implementation of NOW checking accounts in banks and savings and loan associations, the exception, studied the influence of the innovation's perceived radicalness on implementation. They found that 'successful implementation' was less dependent on radicalness than the following four criteria: the existence of flexibility in implementation, a concentration of power somewhere in the organization, the access to technical competence, and management willingness to listen to the staff directly responsible for implementation.[25]

The handful of studies of the implementation of HRM innovations all took place in the public sector. K. E. Marino found that organizational structural variables were related to affirmative action compliance.[26] J. M. Beyer and H. M. Trice studied the implementation of equal employment opportunity and alcoholism policies in government agencies in the Northeast, and found top management inertia and control to be inhibiting factors.[27] Another recent study compared the implementation of the Civil Service Reform Act of 1978 in two agencies, the Environmental Protection Agency and the Mine Safety and Health Administration, and found that differences in strategic position and organizational context affected implementation.[28] At this time, however, it is unclear the extent to which this previous work is generalizable to the private sector, which has a very different employment environment.

Diffusion of Innovation

Research on the diffusion of innovations is commonly viewed as a subset of communication research, which is concerned with "the transfer of new ideas to members of a social system with the objective of bringing about overt behavior change, that is, adoption or rejection of new ideas."[29]

Unfortunately, this definition is limited by its framing of diffusion in terms of either complete adoption or total rejection, rather than in terms of varying levels of acceptance. Additionally, a lot more is known about the diffusion of technical innovations such as NOW checking accounts and telephones than about managerial ones.[30] With the exception of a few notable studies, even less is known about what distinguishes human resource innovations from other managerial initiatives.

R. Walton's work on the diffusion of major work restructuring is significant because of its longitudinal focus and description of the factors influencing adoption across units *within* an organization. He concluded that it is inherently difficult to diffuse work restructuring due to a tension in the piloting unit's relationship with potential adopting units and the lack of sustained top management support.[31]

Unlike Walton's case study approach, the bulk of research on personnel innovations involve large surveys of a number of firms, which count the adoption of a variety of human resource innovations. Two recent studies by R. M. Kanter[32] and F. Schuster,[33] for example, are representative of research in this area, which typically views companies with the greatest number of programs adopted and the earliest date of adoption as the most innovative. The strength of these studies is their focus on the way in which areas of HRM innovation vary across industries and firms. However, consideration of the impact of the innovations on employee behavior—a critical consideration for understanding human resource innovations, or of the influences of properties of the innovations is seldom, if ever, done. Although Company A's quality circle program might be very different in characteristics and motivational impact than the one at Company B, the companies would be considered similar in their innovativeness if the programs were adopted at the same time. Studies such as these tend to treat organizations as "black boxes." We know little about the process by which these innovations were adopted, nor the extent to which they were accepted by members. The crux of understanding HRM innovation is not simply examining where and when a company adopted a new program, but rather investigating the extent to which it has been incorporated into the existing human resources system.

A Pro-Innovation Bias

J. R. Kimberly once observed that the normative question associated with adoption is "How should organizations be structured to foster innovation?" Whereas the diffusion question is "How should innovations be designed and introduced to enhance the rate that they are spread?"[34] It is clear that there are other normative issues as well. The pro-innovation bias of past research has the implication that an innovation *should be* adopted by *all* relevant members of a social system, that it should be rapidly diffused, and that it should neither be re-invented nor rejected.[35] A dramatic example of this influence is offered by research on the use of methadone to "solve" heroin addiction in the 1970s. The phrase "technological fix," an overdependence on technology to solve social problems, is used to describe pro-innovation bias.[36]

Normative issues are especially apropos to the study of human resource innovations. The success of many new work practices aimed at behavior change is dependent on their *voluntary* adoption.[37] Many of the quality circle programs that were adopted in the 1970s and 1980s by Fortune 500 companies have recently been discontinued, perhaps primarily because individuals and groups may not have perceived that they had a choice in adopting the innovation or a say in their design. Perhaps the concept of technological fix is not too distant from the penchant of many U.S. firms in the recent past to search for new HRM technologies such as circles to solve their organizational problems.

Having a pro-innovation bias may be particularly inappropriate for the study of human resource innovations for a more global reason. Aren't the companies that are renowned for managing their employees better known for maintaining steadfast approaches toward their personnel systems (e.g., IBM, Merck) than transient ones? Hasn't there been a general tendency for many Fortune 500 companies to "overadopt"[38] human resource management innovations—the adoption of innovations that should be rejected? Cynical employees might be tempted to refer to this phenomenon as, what Clay Alderfer calls, the "HERWEGA effect," the "Here We Go Again" effect.[39]

The inattention to the issue of rejection or less than complete adoption limits our understanding of organizational responses to "bad" innovations (or mediocre ones) or "good" innovations that were poorly implemented. Our knowledge of why the personnel area is especially fertile for the rapid adoption and discontinuation of copycat programs (e.g., T-groups, quality circles, culture programs), and understanding of how to determine which human resource innovations have the most staying power both would be increased by a study of the extent to which HRM innovations of varying quality are accepted. Issues of quality relate to how well an innovation is adopted and whether sustained implementation occurred, and how quality assessment differs for individuals and groups. However, these areas have received little past scrutiny. In simplistic terms: scholars have framed their question as either ''Was the innovation adopted or rejected?'' or ''Has the innovation spread between organizations, and if so, to what extent?'' The notion that implementation is ''an important phenomenon (not merely noise, error variance, endogenous irrelevance, or individual perversity) has been slow to be incorporated into models of innovation.''[40]

PERSONNEL AND HRM RESEARCH

Cummings once wrote that organizational behavior develops theories and human resources management develops techniques to apply them.[41] Assuming that Cummings's statement is to be taken seriously, his comment helps illuminate the growing need to integrate more organizational behavior theory into personnel research, particularly in terms of examining the systemic impact of human resource innovations. With a few classical exceptions, such as C. T. Argyris's work on T-groups[42] and W. F. Whyte's observations on the group effects of incentive systems,[43] most research has focused on the mechanics of designing and administering a single innovation and has been very narrow in its examination of the impact of new human resource programs.

Consequently, academics often have failed to measure the effect of an innovation such as a new performance appraisal program on other relevant components of the human resource system such as the existing compensation plan and promotion policy. Our understanding of the effectiveness of new human resource programs would be vastly improved if more studies examined selected facets of an entire human resource system's machinery. Taking a holistic view will enable researchers to consider the extent to which other pieces of the human resource system will change to accommodate an innovation as it becomes institutionalized.

Perhaps the historical roots of personnel scholars' piecemeal approach can be traced to the success of the Hawthorne experiments, where managers and researchers found that if they tinkered with the parts (e.g., lighting, temperature, rest periods), short-term acceptance will occur.[44] A cycle was established that encouraged constant innovation with the pieces of the human resource system's machinery. The issue of sustained implementation has been avoided, because the priority has been on introducing something new rather than evaluating the acceptance of old innovations.

Far too many organizations resist systematically collecting empirical data to assess the impact of new HRM programs on employees. Instead, social tests are used to assess program effectiveness, particularly if the standards of desirability are ambiguous.[45] Social tests are those validated by authority or consensus and their validity depends on how many individuals or on who endorses them.[46] Perhaps organizations prefer to rely on external criteria of worth rather than internal criteria. These criteria might include such ceremonial awards as the

Nobel prize, endorsement by important people, the standard prices of professionals and consultants, or the prestige of programs or personnel in external circles.[47] Our understanding of human resource innovation would be greatly enriched if more organizations did not merely rely on social tests to evaluate the effectiveness of new programs, but also examined their social psychological and behavioral impact.

Although a recent *Business Week* article may be entitled "Human Resource Managers Aren't Corporate Nobodies Anymore," the historical tendencies of many organizations to scapegoat their personnel departments and to be led by top executives who give minimal attention to human resource issues also need to be addressed in research on HRM innovations.[48] The tenuous position of HRM departments in many firms may pose an interesting dilemma for personnel managers: "The very fact that the most energetic spokesmen of the human relations approach are themselves subordinates rather than top executives would suggest that they have a strong interest in advocating a view of management which maximizes their own importance in the scheme of things entirely."[49]

If some HRM innovations are adopted merely to promulgate the position of the personnel department, there are obvious ramifications for organizational acceptance.

As for the issue of limited top management involvement, Frederick Taylor's comments drive home the point that executive neglect has historically been a problem: "As a matter of fact, we all know that the great majority of executives have "fallen down" in the human organization of their plants. . . . we executives have treated the question of human organization in our plants as a minor instead of as a major problem."[50] Because organizational issues have traditionally been of secondary importance to line management, perhaps acceptance of human resource innovation is generally going to be more limited a priori than that of technical innovation.

In summary, the human resource management literature has concentrated on the mechanics of designing and administering specific innovations like a new performance appraisal or compensation program. By doing so, however, it often has neglected to study the politics of implementing human resource innovations, the degree to which innovations receive acceptance over an extended period of time, and their relation to other personnel programs and the overall work relations system. Also, the glaring issue that personnel departments traditionally have poor images in their firms and the reality that most top managers are tangentially involved with human resource issues have received cursory attention. This gap can be partially attributed to the lack of interest by organizational development researchers in studying the entire continuum of personnel practices, which has historically been focused only on major innovations such as interventions involving worker participation in decision making. Little research on HRM innovation has been done using theory that integrates the fields of organizational development and personnel.

RESEARCH ON ORGANIZATIONAL DEVELOPMENT
AND CHANGE

Despite the lack of integration between organizational change and personnel research, organizational change and development theory is very useful for understanding HRM innovation. The organizational development process has been defined as "the creation of a culture which supports the institutionalization and use of social technologies to facilitate the diagnosis and change of interpersonal, group, and intergroup behavior."[51]

Although the organizational change caused by a human resource innovation is generally much more modest than the creation of a culture, HRM innovations also can be viewed as social technologies that are employed to create organizational change. If they become institutionalized, they can be viewed as moments in the organizational change process. For example, on the surface the successful introduction of an employee-run newsletter may not be viewed as part of the organizational development process. However, should the newsletter become institutionalized in a traditional hierarchical organization, its acceptance reflects the possibility that major social technologies might be successfully introduced to foster organizational change.

Acceptance of human resource management innovation may *symbolize* that the organization is prepared for major change. Organizational development scholars have written a great deal about organizational culture, and a cultural anthropological analogy is apt. Just as acceptance of a new nutrition program in a primitive culture may prepare the way for the introduction of other technologies, acceptance of a human resource innovation may indicate that the organization is fertile for the initiation of advanced social technologies.

Organizational development theories on resistance to change, the role of the change agent, and the multiple levels of change also have ramifications for understanding innovation acceptance. Shepard once said, "An organization is itself an innovation, but most organizations of the past have been designed to be innovation-resisting."[52] Indeed, much of the work on organizational development has focused on the problems of introducing change into an organization.[53] Lewin's classic three-step procedure of change, which includes unfreezing, movement, and refreezing, can easily be applied to innovation. In order for a human resource innovation to be accepted, employees' current customs must be first unfrozen, then changed, and finally refrozen.[54]

Organizational development theory has also highlighted the importance of examining the differential impact of change on various organizational groups. Views of change may differ according to whether one is (1) a member of the group who is personally affected by a set of events, (2) a change agent who is deliberately attempting to produce new and different responses in members of the group, (3) a group member who is not affected but who observes what may be happening to fellow group members, or (4) an outside observer or historian reconstructing events. Depending on how a given set of events affects us and depending on whether we take a short-range or long-run time perspective, we either see change or continuity.[55]

Perceptions and attitudes toward a personnel innovation are going to differ greatly between individuals, groups, and organizational units depending on where they are in the organizational system. As Alderfer has pointed out in his research on intergroup relationships, there are a variety of perspectives that can be analyzed:

1. The effects on individuals who represent groups in relation to one another.

2. The consequences for subgroups within groups as the groups deal with one another.

3. The outcomes for groups-as-a-whole when they relate to significant other groups.

4. The impact of suprasystem forces on the intergroup relationship in question.[56]

Lastly, many organizational development researchers such as French and Bell[57] have also written on the vital role of the change agent in the OD process. Most HRM innovations are sponsored by a personnel department with low status vis-à-vis other functions. Consequently, consideration of the impact of the personnel department's change agent role on the extent to which the innovation is accepted must be done. It seems likely that there is a relationship between the extent to which a personnel department is respected and the degree to which human resource innovations are accepted by employees.

SUMMARY

Adopting and sustaining progressive human resource management programs is a critical issue facing many organizations today. The systematic evaluation of new personnel programs as organizational innovations has generally not been done by researchers or practitioners. As a consequence, we know little about the conditions influencing the degree to which HRM programs generally take hold in a firm, and we lack a framework for conducting a coordinated evaluation of employee reactions to HRM initiatives.

The study described in this book attempts to fill gaps in our understanding of human resource management innovations in a number of important ways. It examines acceptance of a wider sample of human resource innovations adopted by several large corporate units than any previous research. Employee reactions to multiple HRM programs are analyzed in an effort to consider the influence of employee backgrounds on acceptance. An employee's level in the organizational hierarchy, race, gender, and tenure may have an important influence on attitudes toward and use of personnel innovations.

The study also explores the factors influencing acceptance of HRM innovation across organizational units and various HRM programs, which are viewed as planned organizational innovations. Most of the innovation literature has focused on adoption and diffusion. Whereas some studies have researched evaluation and implementation, little work has been done on the evaluation of human resource innovations in large private sector organizations. Additionally, exploration of a new construct "acceptance of HRM innovation" is done, which has the potential to be used to measure employee perceptions across HRM programs.

NOTES

1. H. H. Heneman, *Research Methodology Needs in Human Resource Management*. Proceedings of the 39th National meeting of the IRRA, New Orleans, December 1986, 252–257.

2. E. E. Lawler, *High-Involvement Management* (San Francisco: Jossey-Bass, 1986), 1.

3. S. M. Jacoby, *Employing Bureaucracy* (New York: Columbia University Press, 1985), 133–65.

4. D. M. Gordon, R. Edwards, and M. Reich, *Divided Workers* (London: Cambridge University Press, 1982).

5. R. Walton and J. R. Hackman, *Implications of Management Strategy for Groups in Organizations*. Paper presented at Carnegie-Mellon conference on groups in organizations, Pittsburgh, 1984.

6. P. J. DiMaggio and W. W. Powell, "The Iron Cage Revisited: Institutional Isomorphism and Collective Rationality in Organizational Fields," *American Sociological Review* 48 (1983): 147–160.

7. A. P. Chandler, Jr., *Strategy and Structure: Chapters in the History of the American Industrial Enterprise* (1962; reprint, Cambridge, Mass.: MIT Press, 1984), Chapter 1.

8. W. R. Nord and S. Tucker, *Implementing Routine and Radical Innovations* (Lexington, Mass.: D. C. Heath, 1987), 6.

9. S. W. Becker and T. L. Whistler, "The Innovative Organization: A Selective View of Current Theory and Research," *Journal of Business* 40 (1967): 463.

10. M. Aiken and J. Hage, "The Organic Organization and Innovation," in Zey-Ferrell, ed., *Readings on Dimensions of Organizations* (Santa Monica, Calif.: Goodyear, 1977), 263–279.

11. E. E. Kossek, "Human Resources Management Innovation," *Human Resource Management* 26, no. 1 (1987): 71–92.

12. G. Zaltman, R. Duncan, and J. Holbek, *Innovations and Organizations* (New York: John Wiley, 1973; reprint, Malabar, Fla.: Robert E. Krieger Publishing), 158.

13. Ibid.

14. G. Klonghan, and W. Coward, Jr., "The Concept of Symbolic Adoption: A Suggested Interpretation," *Rural Sociology* 30 (1970): 77–83.

15. J. R. Kimberly, "Managerial Innovation," in P. Nystrom and W. Starbuck, eds., *Handbook of Organizational Design* (Oxford: Oxford University Press, 1981), 185.

16. G. Downs, and L. Mohr, "Conceptual Issues in the Study of Innovation," *Administrative Science Quarterly* 21 (1976), 700.

17. T. Burns and G. M. Stalker, *The Management of Innovation* (London: Tavistock, 1961).

18. R. M. Kanter, *The Changemasters* (New York: Simon and Schuster, 1983), 200–205.

19. J. Hage, and R. Dewar, "Elite Values Versus Organizational Structure in Predicting Innovation," *Administrative Science Quarterly* 18 (1973), 279–290.

20. T. Caplow, *Principles of Organizations* (New York: Harcourt Brace Jovanovich, 1964).

21. D. Miller, and P. H. Friesen, *Organizations: A Quantum View* (Englewood Cliffs, N.J.: Prentice-Hall, 1984), 277.

22. E. M. Rogers, *Diffusion of Innovations*, 3rd ed. (New York: Free Press, 1983), 363.

23. R. L. Daft, "A Dual-Core Model of Organizational Innovation," *Academy of Management Journal* 21 (1978), 193–210.

24. Rogers, *Diffusion of Innovations*.

25. Nord and Tucker, *Implementing Routine and Radical Innovations*.

26. K. E. Marino, "Structural Correlates of Affirmative Action Compliance," *Journal of Management* 8 (1982), 75–93.

27. J. M. Beyer, and H. M. Trice, *Implementing Change* (New York: Free Press, 1978).

28. G. H. Gaertner, K. N. Gaertner, and D. M. Akinnusi, "Environment, Strategy, and the Implementation of Administrative Change: The Case of Civil Service Reform," *Academy of Management Journal* 27 (1984), 525–543.

29. E. M. Rogers, and F. F. Shoemaker, *Communication of Innovations* (New York: Free Press, 1971), 13.

30. Kimberly, "Managerial Innovation," pp. 84–104.

31. R. Walton, "Establishing and Maintaining High Commitment Work Systems," in *The Organizational Life Cycle* (J. R. Kimberly, R. H. Miles and Assoc.; San Francisco: Jossey-Bass, 1981), 208–290.

32. R. M. Kanter, *The Roots of Corporate Progressivism* (New York: Russell Sage Foundation).

33. F. Schuster, *How Widely Used Are Progressive HRM Practices?* National conference proceedings of the Association of Human Resource Management and Organizational Behavior 1 (Virginia Beach, Va.: Maximilan Press, 1985): 43–47.

34. Kimberly, "Managerial Innovation," pp. 84–104.

35. Rogers, *Diffusion of Innovations*.

36. D. Nelkin, *Methadone Maintenance: A Technological Fix* (New York: George Braziller, 1973).

37. R. Zager, and M. Rosow, *The Innovative Organization: Productivity Programs in Action*, 2nd ed. (New York: Pergamon Press, 1985).

38. Rogers, *Diffusion of Innovations*.

39. C. P. Alderfer, personal communication (1986).

40. L. G. Tornatzky, E. Fergus, J. Avellar, and G. W. Fairweather, *Innovation and Social Process* (Elmsford, N.Y.: Pergamon Press, 1980), 134.

41. L. Cummings, "Towards Organizational Behavior," *Academy of Management Review* (1978), 90–98.

42. C. T. Argyris, "Groups for Organizational Effectiveness," *Harvard Business Review* 42 (1964), 60–67.

43. W. F. Whyte, *Men at Work* (Homewood, Ill.: Dorsey Press, 1961).

44. F. J. Roethlisberger, and W. J. Dickson, *Management and the Worker* (Cambridge, Mass.: Harvard University Press, 1939).

45. J. D. Thompson, *Organizations in Action* (New York: McGraw-Hill, 1967).

46. W. R. Scott, *Organizations: Rational, Natural, and Open Systems*, 2nd ed. (Englewood Cliffs, N.J.: Prentice-Hall, 1987).

47. J. W. Meyer, and B. Rowan, "Institutionalized Organizations: Formal Structures as Myth and Ceremony," *American Journal of Sociology* 83 (1977), 350.

48. J. Hoerr, "Human Resource Managers Aren't Corporate Nobodies Anymore," *Business Week* (Dec. 2, 1985), 58–59.

49. R. Bendix, *Work and Authority in Industry* (New York: John Wiley, 1956; Berkeley: University of California Press, 1974), 334.

50. F. Taylor, cited in Bendix, *Work and Authority*, 299.

51. H. A. Hornstein, B. B. Bunker, W. W. Burke, M. Gindes, and R. J. Lewicki, *Social Intervention: A Behavioral Science Approach* (New York: Free Press, 1971), 5–6.

52. H. Shepard, "Innovation-Resisting and Innovation-Producing Organizations," *Journal of Business*, 40 (1967): 470–477.

53. L. R. Sayles, "The Change Process in Organizations: An Applied Anthropology Analysis," in H. A. Hornstein, *Social Intervention*, 185–195.

54. K. Lewin, "Group Decisions and Social Change," in M. Maccoby, T. Newcomb, and E. L. Hartley, eds., *Readings in Social Psychology* (New York: Holt, Rinehart Winston, 1958), 197–211.

55. M. E. Smith, "The Process of Sociocultural Continuity," *Current Anthropology* 23, no. 2 (1982): 127–142.

56. C. P. Alderfer, "Intergroup Perspective on Group Dynamics," in J. Lorsch, ed., *Handbook of Organizational Behavior* (Englewood Cliffs, N.J.: Prentice-Hall, 1984), 190–222.

57. W. L. French and C. H. Bell, *Organizational Development*, 2nd ed. (Englewood Cliffs, N.J.: Prentice-Hall, 1978).

2

The Organization, Innovations, and Research Strategy

As noted in Chapter 1, a number of important gaps exist in the current body of research on innovation. Most studies have focused on a single innovation, used small samples, and rarely looked at the combined effects of individual, group, and contextual variables.[1] Much of the research on innovation has stressed adoption and diffusion instead of implementation, and consequently, there has been little in-depth study of the events that occur after an innovation has been formally approved for adoption. Little is known about the way in which reactions to innovation differ between key stakeholders in the organization or the factors that have an important impact on the psychological process of acceptance of innovation. Because a lot of the results regarding innovation are based on the study of technological innovation, the extent to which the existing body of theory is relevant to administrative initiatives is unclear. The research strategy was designed to delve into some of the existing gaps in the literature. This chapter contains an overview of the organization, the innovations, and the research methodology.

THE ORGANIZATION

Headquarter employees in the Financial Services (FS) and Data Processing (DP) departments of the Valiant Insurance Corporation (a pseudonym) or VIC, participated in the study. VIC is a nonunion company with a predominately white collar work force, and its corporate offices are located in an urban area in the northeastern United States. It has about 30 thousand employees worldwide with 1985 revenues of approximately $15 billion. The organization is a venerable one, having been in business for over 100 years. As a brochure on the company's history proclaims: "The history of insurance in America reads like a history of (VIC)."

VIC is structured into five groups: National Accounts Marketing, Small Accounts Marketing, Finance, Business Diversification, and Investment. Organizational units from two of the five groups participated in the study. The Financial Services (FS) department of the Small Accounts Marketing Group sells and administers insurance policies to individuals and small businesses. The Data Processing (DP) department is part of the Finance Group. It seeks to ensure that adequate controls are in place and to maximize automation efficiencies.

The departments differed in a number of ways that provided two very different organizational contexts for studying the acceptance of innovation. The size of the headquarters Data Processing department is over twice that of Financial Services. Data Processing has about 2500 employees and Financial Services has about 1000. The split in the percentage of the employee population located in the field versus headquarters differed in each unit. Nearly all of Data Processing's employees participated in the study, as the unit has very few members in the field. In contrast, only a third of Financial Services' total population did, as most of its employees are out in the field. Overall, roughly 10% of VIC's worldwide employee population were part of the research.

Unlike Data Processing, Financial Services had undergone a reorganization during the past year. The reorganization reflects the great environmental uncertainty many financial services groups are experiencing from increasing market competition, squeezed profits, spiraling health costs, and an adverse legal environment. It also illustrates the greater susceptibility of Financial Services to influences from the external environment over Data Processing, which essentially focuses its work internally to serve units within VIC. The levels of acceptance to human resource management innovations might differ between a unit that has recently been reorganized and one that has had no recent change in its reporting relationships.

The departments also differed in their financial operating systems. Financial Services operates as a profit center, whereas Data Processing is a cost center. A profit center operates to generate revenues from the sales of the main products of the organization; a cost center brings no revenues into the firm and charges all of its accumulated costs to profit center units. Thus the primary financial goals differed between the units: Data Processing seeks to minimize costs, whereas Financial Services seeks to maximize profits. These differing objectives might affect the amount of financial resources available to adopt new personnel innovations. Assuming overall organizational profitability, a unit operating as a profit center might have greater financial resources to support new personnel programs than one operating as a cost center.

There are structural differences between the units in the location of the human resources department. In Data Processing, the human resources division is part of the department, which makes the vice president of human resources subordinate to the top executive of the Data Processing department. In contrast, Financial Services is serviced by a human resources unit that implements programs for a number of marketing departments. Consequently, the senior executive of the Financial Services department reports to the same individual as the vice president of human resources for the Small Accounts Marketing Group. These reporting differences might affect the implementation and local ownership of new personnel programs by line management in the two units. A human resource innovation adopted by Data Processing may have received greater scrutiny from the local senior executive than a similar one adopted in Financial Services, simply because the Data Processing head may have been more involved in the process of adopting the innovation, since its initiation was subject to his or her approval.

There are also differences in the nature of the work conducted by the employees and the workers' educational backgrounds in each unit. With the exception of the nonexempt employees who operate the data center, the type of work done by data processing employees generally involves high technology. Even the mail in the Data Processing department is delivered by a computerized cart. Most of the employees have a college education, work with computers, and are in jobs considered to be professional. In contrast, Financial Services has a more diverse population. A third of the employees are in jobs classified as nonexempt, which involve processing paper regarding insurance administration. Most of the nonexempt workers do not need a college degree to perform their jobs. In the same department, however, is also a group of very highly educated individuals who must continue their insurance education at night in order to advance in the actuarial and underwriting divisions.

A final distinction is in the gender ratio of employees. Two-thirds of Financial Services' employees are female, compared to only one-third in Data Processing. All of these differences in the nature of the employee populations may influence the levels of acceptance to human resource innovations.

The departments have a number of similarities. The salary grades are structured into three main groups: officers/managers, professionals, and nonexempt. Many of the human resource policies and practices differentiate between officers/managers and lower groups, providing an important context for this study. The ongoing corporate climate survey program, for example, feeds back data grouped into the three salary grade categories: (1) officers and managers, (2) professionals, and (3) nonexempt. Since officer jobs are not part of the internal job posting system, the salary structure for officer and manager jobs is closed, whereas that for professional and nonexempt jobs is open. No formal absenteeism and turnover

Table 2.1
Employee Statistics by Pay Group and Sex for Financial Services and Data Processing Departments

DEPARTMENT	PAY GROUP	FEMALE		MALE		TOTAL	
		#	%	#	%	#	%
Financial Services	Officer/ Manager	12	15	70	85	82	100
	Professional	162	58	115	42	277	100
	Nonexempt	190	92	45	8	535	100
Data Processing	Officer/ Manager	19	12	153	88	172	100
	Professional	767	38	1252	62	2019	100
	Nonexempt	306	63	182	37	488	100
		1092		1587		2679	

statistics for officers and managers are included in the annual head count report printed by corporate personnel. Executive dining room privileges are available only to officers and managers. Even the United Way campaign reflects this hierarchical split. While on site in September, United Way posters invited employees to contribute money in return for the opportunity to "Dunk an Officer!" into a tub of water.

The officer/management population is predominately male and the nonexempt population is mainly female. Table 2.1 shows August 1986 statistics kept by the company and indicates that 12 of the 82 positions, or 15%, in the officer/manager category in Financial Services, and 19 of the 153 officer/manager positions in Data Processing, or 12%, were held by women. In contrast, 306 out of 488 nonexempt jobs, or 63%, in Data Processing, and 490 out of 535 nonexempt jobs in Financial Services, or 92%, were held by women. The gender ratios for professional jobs were generally more balanced between the sexes; 58% of the professional positions in Financial Services and 38% in Data Processing were held by women.

THE HUMAN RESOURCE MANAGEMENT INNOVATIONS

The innovations studied were: job posting, quality circles, flextime, an employee fitness program, a cash award program to recognize performance, flexible benefits, a peer recognition award, and an employee-run newsletter. These innovations represented a sample of the programs adopted by the company within

Table 2.2
History of Eight Innovations in the United States

INNOVATION	WHEN STARTED	PERCENTAGE OF FIRMS USING
Flexible Benfits	1974, ETS[1], 1978, Amer.Can[2]	8%[3]
Physical Fitness	1894[4], NCR	15%[5]
Flextime	1972, Control Date[6]	15%[7]
Cash Awards	unknown	32%[8]
Quality CIrcles	1970, Smith Kline[9]	36%[10]
	1974, Honeywell & Lockeed[11]	
Newsletter	unknown	36%[12]
Job Posting	1970s	64%[13]
Noncash Awards	unknown	85%[14]

[1]More workers getting a chance to choose benefits cafeteria-style. **Wall Street Journal**, July 14, 1981.

[2]Lund, S. Cafeteria benefits meet changing needs of work force, cut costs. FOCUS, Seattle, Wash., Winter 1982, 2-3.

[3]Ibid.

[4]Wellness & fitness programs. Small Business Report, March 1983, 17-19.

[5]Gorlin, H. Personnel practices III: employee services, work rules. NY: Conference Board, 95, 1985.

[6]Koperlman, R. Alternative work schedules & productivity: a review of the evidence. National Productivity Review, Spring 1986, 150-165.

[7]Gorlin, H. Personnel practices II: hours of work, pay practices, relocation. NY: Conference Board, 92, 1981.

[8]Personnel Management, Bureau of National Affairs, 241:431, 1973.

[9]Price, G. Quality Circles: An approach to productivity improvement, Work in America Institute. New York: Pergammon Press, 1982, 2.

[10]Goodmeasure, Inc., The Changing American Workplace: Work alternatives in the 80s. An AMA Survey Report, 1985, 21.

[11]Crocker, O., Leung Chiu, S., Charny, J.C., Quality Circles. N.Y.: Facts on File, 1982, 27.

[12]Gorlin, H. Personnel practices I: recruitment, placement, training & communication. Conference Board: New York, 1981, 89, 37.

[13]Personnel Management. Bureau of National Affairs, 1978, 207:203.

[14]Ibid.

the past ten years. The organization had no prior experience with any of these programs. Table 2.2 summarizes the use of the innovations studied in the United States. Noncash awards are the most prevalent, and flexible benefits are the most scarce. A brief description of each innovation and relevant findings from previous research are provided below.

The *job posting* innovation, entitled the Job Opportunities Program (JOP), is the oldest of the innovations studied. Adopted in April 1977, it is a system that conspicuously posts throughout the company all nonexempt and lower level professional jobs that cannot be filled by existing staff from within a department, and allows interested employees in the same geographic area to apply for these openings. Although research evaluating job posting has mostly focused on the mechanics of administration,[2] one recent study found employee satisfaction with posting positively correlated with the provision of helpful career counseling to applicants.[3]

Quality circles, which are called Innovation Through Involvement or ITI at VIC, were adopted in November 1983 by Financial Services and in June 1984 by Data Processing. Innovation Through Involvement is a voluntary participative management program that trains employees in problem-solving techniques. Geared mainly toward nonexempt and first-level professional employees, ITI encourages these employees to select problems directly affecting their jobs and to work in teams to develop solutions to present to management. A recent review of over 30 studies on quality circles concluded that circles have had a favorable impact on both individual (e.g., job satisfaction, morale) and organizational (e.g., productivity, quality) outcomes.[4] However, other researchers have raised concerns that some of these results may be spurious, because many of the studies evaluated trial programs that were installed in work units believed to have conditions favoring success and also failed to address possible influences from a "Hawthorne effect."[5]

Flextime was adopted in April 1984. VIC's program consists of flexible working hours where nearly all employees can arrive at work anytime between 7–9 A.M. and can depart between 3:30–5:30 or later. Data center employees are an example of an employee group that is excluded from flextime for reasons of business necessity, since the data center operates three shifts. Research has shown that flextime can have positive attitudinal and behavioral consequences. It has a positive effect on productivity when physical resources are being shared by a work group[6] and can lead to improvements in employee flexibility, work group relations, superior-subordinate relations, and absenteeism.[7]

The *fitness program*, entitled Taking Care, was adopted in July 1985. It is a total health awareness program, which includes: (1) periodic mailings of newsletters with health information to employees, (2) a company fitness center, (3) periodic showing of videos on health issues during lunchtime, (4) the coordination of sessions where employees can meet in groups with others who have similar health needs to discuss how to improve their fitness in a variety of ways, such as quitting smoking, losing weight, exercising at lunch, and taking steps to reduce stress. Although a 1987 review on employee health management programs criticized the rigor of existing research,[8] evidence suggests that fitness programs may improve how long and hard employees work because of increased physical and mental stamina,[9] and can reduce health care costs.[10] However, more research is needed as the majority of respondents to a national survey rated their program's cost/benefit ratio as unknown and indicated that only 40% of employees stay in the programs after their first year despite a program design encouraging participation from all employees.[11]

Initiated in April 1986, The Outstanding Achievement Award Program (TOAAP) is an employee *cash award* innovation for all employees except those on sales or executive incentive plans. It is designed to reward outstanding achievement on the job by a cash bonus of up to a maximum of 15% of an individual's salary. In order to receive the award, an employee must be nominated by his or her manager, who completes a form describing the achievement. Nominations are reviewed by a human resource committee and signed off by a divisional vice president. In some units, the identity of recipients is kept secret. In others, honorees may receive publicity by attending a special meeting where top management presents the award and their pictures are placed on a bulletin board. Research has found that performance-based compensation programs were the most effective when employees participated in their design.[12] Overall, however, limited evaluation research has been conducted specifically on the public awarding of individual cash bonuses to nonmanagerial white collar employees for outstanding performance on the job.

Flexible benefits, entitled the Flexible Spending Account (FSA), were started in May 1986 at VIC. Employees who enroll in this voluntary program have a portion of their paycheck reserved for day care or health expenses not covered by the company benefits package (e.g., eye glasses, plastic surgery etc.). By enrolling, an employee may tax-deduct these expenses. However, if employees do not use all the money they set aside, they lose it. Given the diversity of the design of flexible benefits programs and the fact that the existing literature mainly consists of descriptive case studies,[13] little is known about employee reactions to the programs.

The last two programs were adopted only in the Financial Services department and a literature review yielded no evaluation research that was readily applicable. The *peer recognition program*, the People Are Tops, or the PAT award, was initiated at Financial Services in June 1985. Under this program, employees in the lower salary grades can be nominated by anyone in the department to receive a PAT award for doing a superior job. If the nomination form is favorably reviewed by an employee committee, a recipient will receive a small gift, such as a clock radio, calculator, professional hockey tickets, or a free meal at a local restaurant. The innovation is publicized by posting pictures on each floor showing the recipient shaking hands with a senior executive. Recipients' names are also printed in the employee-run newspaper. Sometimes recipients are notified by gags: a person dressed as a gorilla carrying balloons or an exotic dancer might come to a winner's work area to announce the award. Another feature of the program is an annual luncheon given to reward individuals with perfect attendance.

The *Grapevine*, the *employee-run newsletter*, was started in September 1984. Issued periodically, it is written by employees who were appointed by their divisional vice president to serve as representatives for their functional area. These representatives and other interested employees volunteer to attend occasional meetings during work to plan each issue. Typical features in the newsletter might include irreverent looks at life in Financial Services through jokes and articles that poke fun at work, a front-page folksy article written by a top executive, human interest stories on employee activities, and a point/counterpoint section presenting two sides to a current unsolved work issue (e.g., smoking in the workplace).

RESEARCH STRATEGY

Overview

Alderfer defines diagnostic methodology as "a process based on behavioral science theory for publicly entering a human system, collecting valid data about human experiences with that system, and feeding that information back to the system to promote increased understanding of the system by its members."[14] Given that reactions to HRM innovations are likely to differ greatly between employee groups, diagnostic methodology seems highly appropriate for understanding the extent to which a sample of eight personnel innovations comprising the human resource system of an organization are accepted. It allows the researcher to understand the system on its own terms inductively, rather than impose standardized instruments. The researcher is able to understand some of the "soft" characteristics of human resource innovations as well as the "hard" ones, using a blend of qualitative and quantitative methods that the organization helped choose.

The study was conducted in three phases from June to December 1986. During Phase I, multiple entry meetings were held with senior human resource executives of several departments to discuss the programs to include in the study and to develop a contract letter, employee liaison groups were formed in each department, interviews were held with the managers of the human resource programs, and historical data on the innovations and the organization were collected. Phase II consisted of "empathic questionnaire" development[15] using data from individual and group interviews held with a cross section of employees, and top executive and liaison group review. Phase III included administration of the questionnaire, and written and oral feedback. After the study was completed, a panel of human resource experts rated descriptions of the innovations on a variety of dimensions, which were used to conduct further analysis.

Entry and Phase I

During the first phase, multiple entry meetings were held with senior VIC executives to discuss and finalize the programs included in the study. Based on these meetings, the Financial Services and Data Processing departments agreed to provide financial and organizational commitment to the study and allow data to be collected on six to eight human resource programs that had been introduced in the past decade. Then department liaison groups of seven to eight employees were formed to allow the researcher to interact with a cross section of members and to encourage organizational participation in the implementation of the study.

The formation of liaison groups stems from Alderfer's theory of organizational diagnosis. Because researchers are outsiders, they can be easily prevented from understanding crucial elements of an organization's system.[16] The liaison system assists the researcher in determining "what data to collect, from whom to collect it, when to collect it, and how to collect it."[17]

The senior human resource managers of each department helped the researcher form the liaison groups by providing a list of employees, which varied in terms of functional affiliation, sex, race, age, tenure, and hierarchial status (e.g., officers/managers, professionals, and nonexempt employees). The researcher called each of the suggested individuals and invited them to participate in the liaison group, making it clear that participation was voluntary and that employees should not come to the first meeting if they had any reservations. In addition, one member of each department's senior human resource group was invited to be a liaison member, in order not to isolate them from the study.

The objectives of the first meeting of each liaison group were to introduce the study, to develop a confidential list of employees to invite to participate in group interviews, and to conduct initial examination of employee attitudes on the programs. In regard to the group interviews, another feature of the diagnostic method, members participated in a semi-structured group discussion on each of the innovations, which was recorded with their permission. Members were asked to describe their level of awareness of the innovations, the most salient features of the programs, what they liked and didn't like about how the innovations were administered, and their perceptions of the reasons for the introduction of the innovations.

At the end of the discussion, members were asked to complete an acceptance time line to indicate their perceptions of the way in which their individual attitudes had changed since the programs were introduced. The acceptance time line was designed to help gather initial information on the key employee reactions to the innovations. Members were asked to indicate the level of their initial and current levels of acceptance of the HRM innovations. They also jotted down one or two key factors that influenced the relationship between their initial perceptions and their current ones.

Individual interviews were held with the corporate and local human resource managers who either administered or oversaw the programs. Although the interviews focused on present operations, historical information was also collected because of its ramifications for the current organizational response to the innovations. The managers were invited to give the researcher any written materials on the programs' development and usage and to allow review of existing files, if appropriate.

Because a questionnaire was going to be used in the study and the organization had administered employee opinion surveys in the past, interviews also were held with the head of the corporate opinion survey program and a review of previous surveys was conducted. Data were also collected on absenteeism and turnover rates and the head count for each unit.

Phase II

Phase II consisted of "empathic questionnaire" development using data from interviews, and input from executive and liaison group review of the instrument. An "empathic questionnaire" is written using the language of organizational members.[18] The questionnaire items were developed from individual and group employee interviews, and a page of about 20 items was devoted to each program.

Overall, the questionnaire was designed to measure attitudinal acceptance of each innovation. For each program, there were ten general items comparable across the innovations, which were used to form the acceptance scale that is described in detail in the measures section below. In addition, there were ten items that were uniquely related to the acceptance of each program (sample items: "Flextime has helped people better integrate their working day with the demands of their private lives" and "Overall, the quality circle program has helped make employees more involved in their jobs"). Whereas these empathic items could not be used in quantitative analyses for across innovation comparisons, since they differed for each innovation, they were used to enrich organizational feedback on the study and enhance the researcher's understanding of the results. Also, it is useful to note that interspersing the unique items with the comparable ones on each program's page probably enhanced respondents' motivation to complete the entire questionnaire, despite the repetition of comparable items.

A draft of the empathic questionnaire can be found in the Appendix. The surveys for each department were identical with minor exceptions, such as substituting the words "Data Processing" òr "Financial Services" for various statements, or adding an item at the end of an innovation's section regarding an issue that arose in one liaison group but not the other. In many cases, statements from the group interviews were used to develop items in the language of organizational members.

The survey included positively and negatively worded statements to help guard against a positive response set. The researcher felt a positive response set might be an issue, because in the past the innovation managers had tended to solicit only positive information from the employees in regard to these programs. It was believed that employees might not give responses that reflected their true attitudes toward the programs unless both positive and negative statements regarding the innovations were included on the questionnaire.

The questionnaire also had questions on the working environment, as it was believed that attitudes on the innovations might be influenced by the organizational context in which they are administered. At the end of the survey, employees could report their use of the programs, their backgrounds, and make comments. The background variables included the following: hierarchical level (salary grade group = nonexempt, professionals, officers and managers); race; sex; years with the company (≤ 1, 1–5, 6–10, 11–15, ≥ 16) and program experience (user/ nonuser).

Measures

Attitude toward HRM innovation. For each program, participants completed ten items assessing their attitudes toward personnel innovation using a five-point Likert-type scale (1 = strongly agree; 5 = strongly disagree). Table 2.3 shows a listing of the scale items used to comprise the attitude toward innovation scale.

The scale assessed the following dimensions: (1) the extent to which an individual is familiar with a program, (2) the extent to which the program is important to an individual, (3) the extent to which an individual feels that the program is well run, (4) the extent to which an individual likes the way that it is designed, (5) the extent to which an individual wants to see the program continued, (6) the extent to which an individual believes the program has been effectively communicated, and (7) the extent to which an individual believes his or her immediate supervisor supports the program. The items were developed from a literature review and employee interviews and were summed (reversing negatively worded ones) to measure acceptance of each program. The scale was found to be very reliable across innovation as the reliabilities ranged from .91 to .72. The comparable scales were not strongly correlated (mean r = .19), which suggests that common method variance is not a significant problem and across innovation comparisons can be made.

Phase III

Phase III included questionnaire administration and written and oral feedback. All employees in the two participating units received a letter signed by the top local executive explaining the study's purpose, and a survey with an internal envelope addressed to the researcher. About a week's time was given to return the survey. Oral feedback was given to executives, the liaison groups, and attendees at special departmental meetings. A one-page written feedback sheet was also sent to all employees.

The survey was conducted over several weeks in October. Whereas the survey received no prior publicity in Data Processing, a paragraph describing it was run in the Financial Services employee newspaper about a week prior to distribution. In both departments, each employee received a survey accompanied by a letter signed by a senior executive and an internal envelope addressed to the researcher. The letter for Data Processing was signed by the senior human

Table 2.3
Attitude Toward HRM Innovation Scale

1 = STRONGLY AGREE TO 5 = STRONGLY DISAGREE

<u>STATEMENT</u>

1. I am familiar with the main features of (innovation name).

2. (Innovation name) is very important to me.

3. (Innovation name) has little importance to me.

4. Overall, I think (innovation name) is very well run.

5. A lot of improvement should be made in the way (innovation name) is run.

6. In general, I like the way (innovation name) is designed.

7. My immediate supervisor supports (innovation name).

8. In general, communication on (innovation name) has been good.

9. Overall, (innovation name) is a great program and should be continued.

10. It wouldn't bother me if (innovation name) were discontinued.

resource executive; the Financial Services letter was signed by the senior vice president of the entire department. To employees, this difference in the letter's signature suggested line management was soliciting the evaluation of the innovations in Financial Services, whereas Human Resources was soliciting input in Data Processing. Because the Human Resources division structurally had a different unit head than the other divisions in Financial Services, human resource employees in Financial Services received a letter signed by the vice president of human resources for the Small Accounts Marketing Group. In general, a minimum of a week's time was given to employees to complete the survey in each unit.

The survey administration methodology was chosen in part because data from the interviews suggested that the study might be affected by the generally lukewarm employee response to the firm's on-going opinion survey. The opinion survey is given to a stratified sample of employees every three years. Data from the employee interviews and meetings with the corporate opinion survey staff revealed that some employees do not like going to a separate room to take a survey; feedback sessions are often not well attended and the attendance rate is on the decline; and occasionally less than five employees in significant groups had completed past surveys, which meant that results could not be broken down in a way that wouldn't breach confidentiality.

Consequently, a decision was made to use somewhat different methods of administration in the current study (e.g., census coverage; completion at one's individual time discretion; mail-in return; promise of written feedback to all members). The researcher made it clear in her feedback report, however, that the decision to use different administration methods in no way reflected any criticism of the approach used by the corporate opinion survey department, which had been extremely helpful in allowing her access to their files and insights.

Oral and written feedback sessions were held in December with top management, senior human resource executives, and the liaison groups. Senior executives in the Financial Services and Data Processing departments received lengthy written reports presenting and analyzing the results for their unit and written employee feedback sheets for general distribution. Results by division were also given to each department, so that line management could conduct additional feedback sessions in 1987. The results for the entire survey were also available through departmental human resource representatives.

NOTES

1. J. R. Kimberly and M. J. Evanisko, "Organizational Innovation: The Influence of Individual, Organizational, and Contectural Factors on Hospital Adoption of Technological and Administrative Innovations," *Academy of Management Journal* 24, no. 4 (1981): 689–713.

2. See, e.g., K. J. Kleiman, and L. S. Clark, "Correlations of Employee Satisfaction

with a Job Posting System." Paper presented at the Southeast Psychological Association Convention, New Orleans, (1982).

3. Ibid.

4. M. R. Barrick, and R. A. Alexander, "A Review of Quality Circle Efficacy and the Existence of Positive-Findings Bias," *Personnel Psychology* 40 (1987): 579–592.

5. P. M. Muchinsky, *Psychology Applied to Work: An Introduction to Industrial and Organizational Psychology.* (Homewood, Ill.: Dorsey, 1983), 20–21.

6. D. A. Ralston, W.P. Anthony, and D. J. Gustafson, "Employees May Love Flextime, But What Does It Do to the Organization's Productivity?" *Journal of Applied Psychology* no. 2 (1985): 272–279.

7. V. K. Narayanan, and R. Nath, "A Field Test of Some Attitudinal and Behavioral Consequences of Flextime," *Journal of Applied Psychology* no. 2 (1982): 214–218.

8. R. A. Wolfe, D. O. Ulrich, and D. F. Parker, "Employee Health Management Programs: Review, Critique, and Research Agenda," *Journal of Management* 13, no. 4 (1987): 603–615.

9. R. L. Pate, and S. N. Blair, "Physical Fitness Programming for Health Promotion at the Work-Site," *Preventative Medicine* 12 (1983),632–643.

10. R. J. Shepard, M. Cox, and P. Corey, "Fitness Program Participation: Its Effect on Worker Performance," *Journal of Occupational Medicine* 23 (1981): 359–363.

11. J. N. Kondrasuk, "Corporate Physical Fitness Programs: The Role of the Personnel Department," *Personnel Administrator* (1984), 75–80.

12. E. E. Lawler, *Pay and Organizational Development* (Reading, Mass., Addison-Wesley, 1981), 105–108.

13. See D. Gifford, "The Status of Flexible Compensation," *Personnel Administrator* (May 1984), 19–25, or S. J. Vellerman, "Flexible Packages That Satisfy Employees and the IRS," *Personnel* (March 1985), 33–41.

14. C. P. Alderfer, "The Methodology of Organizational Diagnosis," *Professional Psychology* 11, no. 3 (1980): 459.

15. C. P. Alderfer, and L. D. Brown, "Designing an Empathic Questionnaire for Organizational Research," *Journal of Applied Psychology* 56, no. 6 (1972): 456–460.

16. Alderfer, "Methodology of Organizational Diagnosis," 461.

17. Ibid., 463.

18. Alderfer and Brown, "Designing an Empathic Questionnaire."

3

The History of Adoption of the Innovations

All of these personnel programs have a life cycle.
They either change or die.

> Valiant Insurance Company executive

The current level of organizational acceptance to an HRM innovation is undoubtedly going to be influenced by past events involving its adoption and implementation. Why was the innovation adopted in the first place? What are its formal (and informal) goals? Who are its chief sponsors and owners? How has the innovation been administered? Which individuals and groups has it benefited and which has it hurt? How aggressively was the innovation communicated and how was it positioned to employees? How much organizational support (i.e., dollars, staff, management attention) has it received? Does the innovation have any features similar to past successful innovations? Or unsuccessful ones? How many employees have actually used the innovation? Has it diffused to other organizational units? Has the innovation permeated other aspects of work, or has it mainly existed as a program unto itself? What are the critical events in the innovation's life cycle?

In this chapter, questions such as these are addressed by a synopsis of key events in the history of adoption of each program. Everett Rogers' (1983) model of the innovation process, introduced in chapter 1, is used as a framework to organize our discussion. At the end of the chapter, a comparative analysis of similarities and differences in the history of adoption of each HRM program is provided.

THE JOB OPPORTUNITIES PROGRAM—JOP

Table 3.1 summarizes the innovation process for the Job Opportunities Program (JOP), the oldest program studied. This innovation was implemented by the corporate personnel department in April 1977 in partial response to Equal Employment Opportunity legal pressures. The director of personnel recalled that scrutinization from a government agency regulating affirmative action efforts in firms with major federal contracts prompted the company to initiate job posting. The program was viewed as one means of demonstrating that all employees had equal access to jobs.

The allocation that the government was the prime impetus for adoption is echoed by excerpts from a July 1976 memo from an executive to the senior vice president of personnel: "As you know, the commitment to job posting was made because of an agreement with the Social Security Administration Compliance Staff to have such a program in place before 1978. While the initial reaction of the Company was one of reluctant agreement, we are now convinced that job posting will be good for VIC and its employees."

The memo also outlined additional, more positive rationales for implementing job posting, which were cited in the 1977 official JOP announcement from VIC's president to all management employees. The official objectives of job posting were: (1) to encourage individual initiative in the selection and direction of careers, (2) to more effectively utilize the company's human resources, as previously hidden valuable workers will be able to apply for jobs that they had not been aware of in the past, (3) to reduce turnover by improving the chances for career changes within the company, (4) to make clear the variety of opportunities within the organization and the skills and abilities required, and (5) to assist in the achievement of our affirmative action goals.

Before implementing job posting, members of the corporate human resources staff investigated programs at other companies in the financial services industry. They asked other firms: "Now that you have this program in place, was it a good idea?" With this information and full knowledge of VIC's own situation, the managers developed a proposal for corporate headquarters using a sampling of the best features of these programs. The proposal was presented to key personnel and line management people from around the company in order to gain consensus and to make minor modifications. Several years later, the corporate human resources staff would go back to these same people and ask them, "What would you change?" Basically, the (adoption) process that VIC would develop for flextime would be modeled after what the corporate staff had done for job posting.

Once consensus on the design of job posting was gotten from the internal

Table 3.1
Stages in the Job Posting Innovation Process

STAGE	DATE	MAJOR ACTIVITIES
I. INITIATION:		
1. AGENDA-SETTING	'76:	VIC signs affirmative action consent decree.
2. MATCHING	'76:	VIC investigates job posting programs adopted at 12 other insurance companies.

- - - - - - - - - - - - - - - The Decision to Adopt- - - - - - - - - - - - - - -

	7/76:	Job posting proposal approved by the Senior Vice President of Human Resources
II. IMPLEMENTATION:		
3. REDEFINING/ RESTRUCTURING	8/76:	Job posting procedures reviewed by Human Resource representatives from departments.
	12/76:	Presentation made to line managers.
	1/77- 3/77:	Chairman announces job posting in bulletin to all employees. Articles on job posting appear in company newspaper.
	4/77:	Job posting implemented at headquarters. Booklet entitled, "You and Your Salary" sent to all employees.
	10/77:	Job posting implemented at field locations.
4. CLARIFYING	'85:	Rule for notifying supervisors of subordinates' interest in job posting changed to include only candidates who are selected for interviews. Corporate Personnel surveys department representatives on whether the rule that applicants must be in a job at least 6 months before posting should be extended to 1 year, on whether posting between different geographic locations should be allowed, and on whether limits should be placed on the number of salary grades a successful applicant can jump from his/her old job to a new one.
5. ROUTINIZING	'85:	Corporate Personnel sponsors a task force to revisit the entire program. Should the time in job rule be extended from 6 to 12 months? Should job posting be expanded to include manager and officer levels? Should job posting be computerized as a way of decreasing the amount of time it takes to fill vacancies?

managers who would be most affected by its adoption, a variety of implementation measures were taken. Orientation sessions were conducted for all VIC supervisors, a series of articles appeared in the company newspaper, and a booklet was prepared for all employees entitled "You and Your Salary."

The job posting program was a radical innovation for VIC. Its implementation at the corporate headquarters required the making of the transition from a closed salary system to an open one for all positions except those of officers, which comprised the highest level salary group. The adoption of job posting prompted the first public discussion of the salary system, which was historically "a culturally taboo topic." The magnitude of job posting's impact on the entire human resource system is underscored by an excerpt from a 1977 memo written by a personnel manager to line managers: "This program is considered to be the most significant personnel-related change at VIC since the initiation of our formalized pension plan in 1954."

The general mechanics of job posting are relatively straightforward. When a vacancy occurs, interested candidates from within a unit are first reviewed as possible contenders for the job. If there are no suitable internal candidates, the vacancy is announced throughout the corporate offices. Once a week, openings for professional and nonexempt jobs are posted at 16 locations around headquarters. The corporate personnel counselors prepare a list of up to five people eligible for interviews, which is forwarded to the local personnel department. Then the hiring manager gets to pick the candidates to interview from the list. There are only two reasons that persons can be omitted from interviews: (1) Their background does not meet the job requirements, or (2) there is a better qualified candidate. All supervisors of any person chosen for an interview are notified of their subordinate's interest in the vacancy, even if the candidate is not ultimately chosen for the job.

When job posting was first adopted, however, *all* supervisors were notified that their subordinates were posting, even if they didn't receive interviews. As a personnel director recalled, "Some supervisors were shocked to hear their subordinates were unhappy. Because of this, we now notify only those supervisors whose employees are interviewed."

If an employee is selected to fill the opening, typically at least two weeks' notice is given to his or her supervisor. If no suitable candidates emerge through job posting, then the supervisor is allowed to hire from outside the company. With minor modifications, a job posting program similar to the one adopted at headquarters was implemented in many field offices in October 1977.

The changing of the supervisor notification rule is an example of an action occurring in the clarifying stage of the innovation process, "where the relationship between the innovation and the organization is defined more clearly as the innovation is put to full and regular use."[1] Some other issues that required clarification were: (1) how long does an employee need to be in a job before posting—should the six months' rule be increased to a year? (2) how many salary grades can an employee jump from his or her old job to the new job? (3) can there be interoffice posting between two different geographic locations?

Whereas issues such as these might seem mundane to an outside observer who is not concerned with the intricacies of job posting, they currently are being revisited by a task force. Under the direction of a corporate personnel director, the task force was formed in 1987 "because we wanted to look at the whole thing rather than pieces of it." The task force will also discuss whether jobs at the officer level should be posted, and the costs and benefits of computerizing the posting process in order to decrease the amount of time it takes to fill a job. This time lag problem is a live issue for many employees; however, a more critical implementation issue relates to the credibility of the system. Some employees believe that many times the jobs are already spoken for before people even post and the personnel department just goes through the mechanics of posting.

At a local level, there is an important difference in the way that job posting is implemented in Data Processing versus Financial Services. In Data Processing, the human resources staff maintains a separate system for Data Processing employees only, which gives departmental employees first shot at openings. Although Financial Services used to have a separate posting system for its employees, the local program was discontinued after the reorganization. A human resources executive commented, "I'm not sure there was a design to do it. It just happened. Internal posting works when you have relatively closeknit employees. It doesn't work when you have a department spread all over."

Consequently, openings in Financial Services are posted immediately in the corporate system, whereas openings in Data Processing are posted within the department one week before they are posted corporately. According to the human resources director who oversees job posting in Data Processing, "Ninety-eight percent of Data Processing's jobs are filled from within the department." He believes the main reason Data Processing has a separate system is "efficiency," and the competitiveness and volatility of the labor market for technical data processing personnel, which has high turnover. The longer that a Data Processing person is left discontent, the greater the chance the individual will go somewhere else for $15,000 more. Data Processing needs are intimately understood by department job counselors who can react immediately to them. The competitiveness of Data Processing's labor market is highlighted by the fact that they are the only department with a "Grab a friend, grab a grand" recruiting incentive program, which encourages employees to recruit friends for positions in Data Processing. It appears that external environmental pressures have led to the tailoring of an innovation to effectively meet local needs.

QUALITY CIRCLES: INNOVATION THROUGH INVOLVEMENT

If the volume of paper generated by an innovation was indicative of the level of its impact, Innovation Through Involvement (ITI), the quality circle program, could be viewed as the one having the greatest influence on employees; it has generated the greatest number of historical files of all the innovations studied. However, unobtrusive measures do not always reflect reality.

Innovation Through Involvement was initiated at VIC in 1983, partially as a result of a senior employee's attendance at an industry conference in 1982 where he heard a presentation on quality circles. According to the coordinator of ITI in Financial Services, the attendee thought quality circles might "address the chairman's interest in derobotizing employees and getting them more involved in their work." When the employee returned from the conference, he shared materials on quality circles with senior staff members in the corporate training department.

One of the corporate trainers (who has since been anointed with the title of "the Patron Saint of Quality Circles") spoke to her boss about the possibility of implementing quality circles at VIC. The patron saint's boss in turn got permission from his boss, the senior vice president of human resources, to hire a consultant in order to address the chairman's interest in the innovation. In retrospect, the patron saint proclaimed: "I don't know why my boss did it. It was so out of character!" With the senior vice president's blessing, the corporate training department began a search for a consultant and hired "the only one who could think—he didn't just come in with his overheads and canned presentation." Several months later, the consultant led a corporate-sponsored session on the concepts of Innovation Through Involvement, where "the chairman gave people the opportunity to buy into the program or not buy into the program."

Quality Circles in Financial Services

As the summary of the quality circle innovation process in Table 3.2 shows, Financial Services was the first department to implement ITI in April 1984, and was followed by Data Processing eight months later. It has been suggested that one reason Financial Services was the first unit to adopt ITI was because they were represented at the corporate meeting by their senior human resources executive and not their senior operating executive, who was too busy to attend.

One explanation for Financial Service's speedy implementation is that they were the only unit that had previously experimented with other forms of the innovation: a participative management program called Productivity Through Job Involvement (PJI), which formed work unit groups to allow for increased communication and discussion among members. Indeed, some skeptical employees viewed ITI as another fad replacing PJI. It was just another way for management "to show the grunts they care" and also to be competitive with other companies.

There may be some truth to the contention that ITI mainly was adopted somewhat faddishly. As one personnel director who helped initiate ITI in Financial Services recalled, "A lot had been written about this and we said, 'Let's try it.' Once it started, it moved quickly. The Innovation Through Involvement pin came out of the book on excellence. No one had a pin before at VIC."

The coordinator of quality circles for Financial Services, who is subordinate to this director, believes the reason his department was the first VIC unit to adopt quality circles was not only due to media hyperbole, but also organizational culture. Financial Services views itself as being very people-oriented, easy-going, and laid back; its style of management is to let people make mistakes. There was also a question of turf and prestige, as the initiation of ITI gave Financial Service's senior vice president bragging rights. This sanguine description of Financial Services' management style differs from the one given by a human resources executive who is senior to the quality circle coordinator: ''The insurance industry (i.e., Financial Services) is not a good place for quality circles—it's too control-oriented.''

What exactly was the VIC brand of quality circles? A Financial Services brochure defined ITI as: ''small groups of people who volunteer to meet regularly on company time to identify, analyze, and solve problems related to their work. ITI is a participative management approach to decision making and problem solving which capitalizes on the imagination and resourcefulness of employees by using a work process, which we believe occurs everyday.''

Although Innovation Through Involvement was initiated by the same consultant in Data Processing and Financial Services, there are many differences in its implementation, because ownership of the innovation lies at the department level. Each department printed its own pamphlet signed by its senior line manager, which was tailored to its local audience. Financial Service's cover has a remark by its senior line manager: ''Though we may be better than we were yesterday, we are not as good as we must become.'' The cover of Data Processing's brochure has the statement, ''Capturing the creativity of the individual and the synergy of the group.'' (Unlike Financial Services, most of the work in Data Processing is done in teams.)

The inside of each pamphlet lists different goals for ITI. Financial Services' goals are to:

1. Do our jobs better by effectively utilizing all our resources.
2. Improve communication between all employees in all divisions.
3. Improve our ability to plan for change.
4. Commit to a longer-term effort to develop the whole person.
5. Create a stronger problem-solving atmosphere.

The objectives of Data Processing's circles are:

1. Give you a forum for presenting your ideas to management.
2. Gain your support and commitment to changes in the workplace.
3. Teach you innovative approaches to problem solving.
4. Increase your involvement in decision making.
5. Propose new ideas that reduce our cost of doing business.
6. Increase real participation in contributing toward achievement of corporate goals.
7. Provide the means for using our resources more effectively.

Table 3.2
Stages in the Quality Circle Innovation Process

STAGE	DATE	MAJOR ACTIVITIES
I. INITIATION:		
1. AGENDA-SETTING	'82:	VIC sends employee to Quality Circle Conference.
2. MATCHING	12/82:	The Senior Vice President of Human Resources encourages the Training Department to interview Quality Circle Consultants.

- - - - - - - - - - - - - - - The Decision to Adopt- - - - - - - - - - - - - - -

	DATE	MAJOR ACTIVITIES
	6/83:	Quality Circle Consultant hired by VIC's Corporate Training Department.
II. IMPLEMENTATION:		
3. REDEFINING/ RESTRUCTURING	9/83:	Consultant leads off site orientation session for Financial Services Management.
	11/83:	Financial Services appoints a steering committee and a coordinator.
	1/84:	Financial Services sends an announcement to all employees inviting them to an orientation and meeting on Quality Circles.
	2/84:	Financial Services holds two orientation meetings: a closed session for middle management and a fireside chat that is open to all employees.
	3/84:	Financial Services selects and trains facilitators and leaders for Circles.
	4/84:	Twenty-eight Circles begin meeting in Financial Services. Financial Services Circles Newsletter begins. Consultant leads orientation session for Data Processing Management.
	6/84:	Data Processing appoints a steering committee and coordinator.
	11/84:	Data Processing holds orientation session for all employees.
	12/84:	Twelve Circles begin meeting in Data Processing. Data Processing Circles leaders trained.

Table 3.2 (continued)

STAGE	DATE	MAJOR ACTIVITIES
	3/85:	Data Processing Circle Newsletter begins.
4. CLARIFYING	8/84:	First Circle makes management presentation in Financial Services.
	9/84:	Consultant and Patron Saint Lead Process audit of Financial Services' Quality Circles. Financial Services coordinator and Steering Committee asked to clarify implementation issues. Are Circle suggestions eligible for the corporate suggestion plan? Is the training for Circle leaders too long? Should supervisors be allowed to join Circles?
	5/85:	Expansion to 35 Circles in Financial Services
	11/85:	First Circle makes management presentation in Data Processing.
		Expansion to 24 Circles in Data Processing
		Data Processing coordinator and Steering Committee clarify implementation issues. Should middle management participate more by forming their own Circles? Can Circles select problems affecting more than their own work area?
	1/86:	Reorganization in Financial Services disrupts the operation of established Circles.
		Program officially expands to 40 Circles in Financial Services.
	2/86:	Financial Services' Steering Committee has confrontative meeting with consultant.
		Consultant and Patron Saint hold Circle Process audit in Data Processing.
		Official number of Financial Services Circles declines to 35.
	3/86:	Official number of Financial Services Circles declines to 21.
	5/86:	Small Account Marketing group management plans to expand circles to units other than Financial Services.

Table 3.2 (continued)

STAGE	DATE	MAJOR ACTIVITIES
	8/86:	Official number of Data Processing circles increases to 45, which includes circles at remote locations.
	9/86:	Data Processing Circle wins eastern regional competition of the International Association of Quality Circles.
5. ROUTINIZING		

A key difference between the stated objectives is Data Processing's mention of the goal of reducing financial costs; Financial Services is silent on the issue. As a memo from a senior human resource executive to line management in Financial Services explained the department's philosophy: "From the outset we agreed that we should not attempt to trace results to the bottom line too early. We should use the number of circles formed, the number of individuals who volunteered, the number. . . . who went through the basic cycle, leader and facilitator training, and subsequently, the number of management presentations made as measures of success."

In Financial Services, the implementation process began with presentations made by the consultant to local line management where they were given an opportunity to commit financial and conceptual support to the innovation. Then a steering committee, which mainly consisted of members of top management, was formed and a coordinator was chosen. When asked why he was selected for the job, the coordinator said it was because he had good people skills and had controversial assignments in the past. When given the same question, the coordinator's boss answered that the steering committee selected the coordinator because he was viewed as being very personable up and down the organization and good at dealing with people who don't necessarily report to him, even though he wasn't considered a good manager. Besides it also helped that he played tennis and softball with the top line manager of the department.

Two months after the steering committee met, an announcement was sent from the senior vice president of Financial Services to all employees inviting them to volunteer for Innovation Through Involvement. Then a four-hour middle management orientation session was held. Next, employee orientation sessions or "fireside chats" given by members of the senior executive's staff were held during the lunch hour. Leaders and team facilitators were chosen from the employee sign-up sheets and 23 circles were initiated in April 1984. A newsletter was also started to publicize the activities of the quality circle teams, which had such names as "Actuarials Anonymous," "the Loan Sharks," and "TeamWORKS." By August 1984, the first circle made a management presentation on how to improve the distribution of secretarial work by developing a color coding system to prioritize each job's urgency.

In September a "process audit" of Financial Services' quality circles was conducted by the patron saint and the consultant, which highlighted a number of areas for improvement. Management needed to demonstrate their commitment to Innovation Through Involvement more visibly. Also, the position of the ITI coordinator needed to be strengthened to allow him to act as a liaison between the teams and the steering committee. Training needed to be conducted for some team leaders who had not yet been through the formal program. But, most importantly, the audit noted that the overall "mission" or reason for the existence of the quality circles program needed to be more clearly formulated and understood by the whole organization.

A number of other issues arose during implementation of the circles that required clarification as well. Does the leader training take too long to complete, as some teams that were started up after the initial startup were being led by people who hadn't completed all training modules? Should participation in quality circles be noted on employees' personnel files? (By 1986 a decision was made to give all participants a citation on their files.)

Should supervisors be team leaders? The steering committee initially thought so, but soon allowed employees who weren't supervisors to be chosen leaders, in response to employee sentiments voiced at the orientation session. However, the issue of supervisor involvement remained unresolved. The minutes of a steering committee meeting held during winter 1984 indicated that some supervisors were reluctant to go near a circle meeting, because they felt the quality circle authority structure competed with their own.

Are suggestions from ITI eligible for the employee suggestion plan? In October 1985, the corporate committee overseeing the suggestion plan voted to give each member of the first team that had a proposal accepted by management a whopping $8.75 for the suggestion. By June 1986, however, the suggestion committee reversed itself and decided to separate all ITI suggestions from the employee suggestion plan. According to the corporate suggestion plan administrator, the committee felt that suggestions made through participation in quality circles should be considered part of an employee's job, and therefore exempt from the suggestion plan. In effect, the innovation failed to permeate the most established participative management component of the human resources system, the suggestion plan, which had been in place since 1946—over four decades.

These clarifying problems reached a head in February 1985, when Financial Services' management brought the consultant into their unit for the last time. It was clear that things had not been going well and were not happening according to plan. Circle meetings were taking too much time, and management was losing support for the program. The steering committee placed a lot of blame for the program's problems on the consultant.

The consultant, on the other hand, perceived Financial Services' management to be the problem. They weren't willing to spend the bucks to support the program. Also, the rubber was starting to meet the road and they were beginning to have to handle the day-to-day realities of the program. Financial Services had a steering committee that didn't meet often enough, a coordinator who was ineffective and didn't give enough time to the program, and they started too many teams at once.

Despite this confrontation, the consultant returned with the sponsorship of the patron saint in April to lead a corporate session on sociotechnical design with the same ''join if you wish'' format similar to the one used for ITI. He and a friend from a sociotechnical consortium wanted to entice Financial Services management to move one step beyond ITI and implement their latest participative management program, SCAN, which is based on sociotechnical design. Although Financial Services management attended the presentation, they didn't volunteer to adopt this latest innovation in participative management.

Their hands were full with the wholesale rejection that ITI was beginning to receive in the unit. All five circles in the customer services division, for example, were inactive. An April memo to the quality circle coordinator observed that the level of enthusiasm of members ranged from little to intense bitterness. The main cause was attributed to lack of support at the supervisor/manager level. For instance, although a circle presentation made in May 1985 was approved, implementation resulted in numerous confrontations between circle members and management. Several managers had attended a circle meeting uninvited and unannounced to publicly attack and reprimand the circle leader. There were numerous other instances of animosity between circle members and supervision (both ITI and non-ITI-related). All members felt that morale had worsened, their jobs were jeopardized, and that any further participation in the ITI program would label them as troublemakers with current management.

Senior members of human resources management also were continuing to worry about the health of Innovation Through Involvement, as illustrated by an excerpt from a May 21 memo from the top human resources executive to the head of the marketing department: ''Keeping the program alive will be difficult unless it is implemented in other parts of the marketing group. If it is to retain its health, we will need to expand the program to other segments of your group. I suggest a presentation to your key staff outlining the program. Since we have a steering committee in place, we could proceed rapidly. The benefits during this period of change could be substantial.''

Not interested in expanding immediately and probably not aware of the potential for replicating R. Walton's ''diffuse or die'' theory,[2] where he found that the failure to diffuse a work restructuring innovation from the Topeka plant to other parts of the corporation had a detrimental effect on the health of the innovation in the pioneer unit, the head of the marketing group did not support the recommendation for immediate expansion. Although he had no concerns about the long-term benefit of ITI and its expansion, the senior executive felt that the current timing was poor for expansion, in light of the reorganization that was going to occur over the next six months. He preferred to plan expansion after whatever disruption occurred because of the reorganization. He also did not agree with the corollary that failure to proceed further in the marketing group at this time puts a "cloud" over progress in Financial Services.

Despite these dismal private communications, the growth in the official number of circles continued with peak expansion to 40 circles in June 1985, which involved about 30% of all Financial Services employees. However, only 28 of those 40 circles were active. Although 15 of the original 23 circles had made management presentations and had their proposals officially accepted, the urgency of management follow-up on implementation varied widely between divisions.

External to the organization, however, Financial Services began proudly publicizing that it was on the cutting edge of the innovation by becoming members of the local chapter of the International Association of Quality Circles (IAQC). A Financial Services competition was scheduled where four teams competed to have the honor of representing VIC at a regional conference of the International Association of Quality Circles. (Not all employees enjoyed the competition, as some participants found it "demoralizing.")

The coordinator and his assistant became officers in the local chapter of the International Association of Quality Circles, and periodically sent memos to circle leaders and facilitators to invite them to the monthly meetings. (In concert with VIC's strict hierarchial management style, team members generally were not invited to the monthly meetings.) At the end of 1985, a memo from the human resources vice president to all Financial Services employees extolled the results of ITI: "We have shared our training techniques with the Group Pensions and Data Processing departments, and provided consulting services to . . . J. C. Penny, Monsanto, Friendly's. Through our efforts . . . VIC is viewed as a leader in quality circles and employee participation in the Northeast."

In January 1986, Financial Services experienced the major reorganization that the senior line executive knew was in the works. In retrospect, the consultant felt that ITI was poorly managed during the reorganization, because Financial Services management didn't use the teams in the reorganization process. The teams could have provided input on the design of the reorganization or new teams should have been structured around the new organizational boundaries. In essence, management viewed the innovation as being separate from the day-to-day work of running the business!

Senior Financial Services management, on the other hand, blamed the reorganization for the growing rejection of ITI. As an executive commented, "We are currently experiencing a change in employee enthusiasm for the program, which I believe can be traced to the reorganization. Many of our people have new jobs, or the very least, a new boss or location . . . We will not be launching a big effort for expansion within marketing during 1986."

Despite this mention of planned expansion, the innovation never became routinized in Financial Services, as it began the process that innovation researchers refer to as "exnovation," when innovations die.[3] No newsletter was sent out since January 1986. The steering committee hadn't met since February 1986. In an October 1986 interview, the senior line executive said "Innovation Through Involvement was a good program, but now it's on its way down. I don't know why it failed. Maybe we didn't support it enough."

Quality Circles in Data Processing

Although a similar implementation process was generally followed in Data Processing, there are key differences. Despite its larger size, in April 1985, Data Processing began only half the number of circles as Financial Services did at startup. Instead of initially opening up participation to all employees, members of the steering committee approached division managers who were viewed as being the most receptive to participative management and asked them to support the founding circles. Unlike Financial Services' bottom-up recruitment approach, Data Processing's approach was top-down. The ITI coordinator for Data Processing explained: "I don't go into an area and say, everyone can sign up in a circle. I want circles formed with people who have something in common."

Unlike Financial Services, Data Processing trained the team members *first* to help the teams form, and then the leaders and facilitators. Data Processing supervisors are given the right of refusal to be team leaders, before other employees can be chosen to lead circles. Data Processing also started a middle management circle very early in the program, which later disbanded after the senior line executive rejected their proposal for increased management training. The ITI coordinator in Data Processing felt that the reason for the rejection was merely a matter of poor timing, as the top executive reviewed the proposal just after he had gotten off a helicopter. She believes that eventually the executive will approve more management training, but its installation may not be marketed as part of the ITI system.

In contrast, Financial Services did not have any activity at the middle management level, mainly because the senior line executive felt this would be an example of top-down instead of bottom-up participation; and also because "I thought they would fail, because in the end, the middle and senior managers wouldn't have time to attend the meetings."

The individual selected to oversee the implementation of quality circles in Data Processing was a seasoned senior employee who was brought in from the field in January 1984. This individual, a director, chose an enthusiastic former schoolteacher to coordinate ITI, who maintains, "I don't think we've had a major downturn in the program yet."

Circle membership differs between the departments. In Financial Services most of its circles involve clerical employees who do not have college degrees, whereas in Data Processing most of its circles involve technical personnel, many of whom are college-educated. Due to differences in job content, the issues selected for problem solving by Data Processing circles are generally more complex than those selected by Financial Services circles, as they are usually related to computer technology and systems design. Consequently, the amount of time to go through the circle cycle is much longer in Data Processing. In November 1985, six months after forming, the first circle made a presentation on the development of career paths for DP trainers. That same month, 12 new circles were also formed. (Financial Services' time period for the first management presentation was two months.)

During implementation, the main issues requiring clarification in Data Processing were: (1) should middle management participate more? and (2) should a circle be allowed to take on problems affecting more than one area? Unlike the earlier process audit that the patron saint and consultant had conducted in Financial Services, the audit for Data Processing in February 1986 contained praise for the coordinator and the recommendation that the steering committee needed to reaffirm their commitment and increase their visibility. By August 1986, 45 circles had been formed, including three at a remote data processing center in Georgia. In September, a Data Processing group won the International Association of Quality Circle's eastern competition. Eight management presentations had been made compared with 15 for Financial Services.

Despite the smoother initial adoption of ITI in Data Processing, it is not clear whether the innovation will become institutionalized in the department. Data Processing's program is eight months newer than the one in Financial Services, and organizational learning may have occurred where Data Processing benefited by hearing about some of the mistakes that Financial Services made in startup. As Ed Lawler, a leading scholar in participative management, points out, most quality circles fade over time because management views them as separate programs.[4] This view is echoed by a DP director: "The key indicator of how successful Innovation Through Involvement is, is when it becomes part of the normal management process and not a separate program that does not mesh and interface with other programs."

However, it appears that commitment from top management in Data Processing may not be sufficient to allow ITI to spread throughout the entire Data Processing organization. When asked about the senior executive's support of quality circles, for example, the coordinator for Data Processing said: "He let it happen. He didn't actively support it, but let it happen." The less than overwhelming support of the top executive for ITI is echoed by data from a January 1987 kickoff meeting, which the researcher attended to give a feedback presentation. The senior executive, who was also a speaker, entered at the minute of his scheduled speech and turned to the coordinator in front of the quality circle leaders in attendance and said, "Now what is it you want me to talk about?" After the session, the coordinator said to me, "You see what I have to deal with sometimes."

THE FITNESS PROGRAM

In 1927 VIC company doctor Ralph Filson wrote, "I am sure that much of the distress occasioned by sickness and a great number of premature deaths could be avoided if the mass of people were only shown and taught how to protect themselves against disease and how to live to keep themselves fit. We have an opportunity to sponsor a worthwhile objective, 'the intelligent spreading of the Gospel of Health.' Everyone should be in the fold 'swearing allegiance to the flag of Health.' ''

As the preceding excerpt demonstrates, employee fitness and health care have been concerns of VIC managers for many decades. In recent years the problem of health care cost escalation had evolved into a critical strategic issue for insurance companies. During the 1970s, health care costs began rising about 13% per year and in the 1980s, they started skyrocketing to about an 18% increase per year.[5] Facing increasing competition for market share, VIC chartered a cost containment project team in the Group Insurance department in 1978. As Table 3.3 shows, its mission was to study issues of health care cost escalation and to develop solutions to help service existing customers and attract new ones. By 1980 a variety of cost containment products were developed under the name the Contain program, which VIC began offering to customers.

By mid–1982 a proposal was made by the Group Insurance department to implement the Contain program, and a corporate committee on health care cost containment was formed in 1983 to oversee it. With this decision to implement the program in-house at a cost of $100,000 per year, it was determined that VIC should be not only a *creator*, but also a *consumer* of innovation in the health care cost containment area. As the Contain committee chairman put it, "We asked ourselves, Where's the laboratory? Should we apply the same programs to our employees that we market to our customers?"

Concurrently, VIC also modified its employee health care benefits package by increasing the level that employees contributed to pay their health expenses. This was the first increase in the amount employees contributed to the coverage of their health expenses since 1971, and a second increase was planned to begin in 1984. VIC also initiated a second opinion surgery program, called Patient Advocate, as a means of avoiding or minimizing hospital or surgical expenses. (Whereas the details of this latter program are not examined here, it is interesting to note that some employees interviewed referred to it as "Patient Aggravate.")

In 1983 VIC adopted Taking Care as part of the Contain program. Taking Care is a comprehensive employee communication program designed to promote positive lifestyle practices and medical self-care whenever possible. A product of a VIC subsidiary, Taking Care includes an initial health appraisal of each employee, a Taking Care self-help bible, monthly mailings of newsletters to employees' homes, and the running of periodic health focus activities.

The decision to implement Taking Care at VIC triggered some key implementation issues that the head of the Contain committee highlighted in a 1984 report to the chairman:

1. Should VIC show increased commitment to Taking Care by hiring a full-time director?
2. Should VIC *lead* or *lag* in the area of health care cost containment innovation?

3. If VIC wants to lead, should more resources be devoted to the program?
4. How should its success be measured?

Having made the following statement in 1983: "America has the most comprehensive, sophisticated—and expensive health care system in history," the chairman of VIC was very receptive to approving additional organizational support for Taking Care. A director of Taking Care was hired in 1985, who had in his words, "a mission from God." This expert in corporate health care promotion was brought in from Xerox, an early leader in the area of employee fitness programs. Most companies usually build a fitness center first and start educating their employees on how to live healthier lifestyles second. According to the Taking Care director, this approach generally results in only about 20% utilization of the center. Consequently, he will spend a little less than a million dollars a year to educate employees *first* on fitness and *then* build a fitness center.

The chairman approved funds to support the building of the "biggest and best fitness center in corporate America" at a cost of $3 million initially, and an estimated $1 million a year to maintain. Open to all employees with at least one year's tenure, the director and his newly hired fitness center manager began giving "employee dog and pony shows" in June 1986, which were followed by an employee sign-up period a month later. Interested employees have to go through an extensive examination in order to receive approval to use the center, which is scheduled to open in the fourth quarter of 1986, and must also show financial commitment by paying an annual $100 fee and the one-time costs of a physical. Three Taking Care mini-centers are also scheduled to open at several field locations in 1987. As the Taking Care director points out, "This is a giant step up from only having a small rumpus room near the executive dining room."

In order to prove the effectiveness of Taking Care, the director has hired educational researchers to evaluate its impact on employee benefits usage. Benefits use and attitudes toward Taking Care and fitness in general will be tracked for 1000 employees from 1986 to 1989. It is hoped that the evaluation will show that Taking Care has helped employees meet a number of objectives: (1) make more informed decisions about the use of professional health care services, (2) develop self-care skills for most minor illnesses, (3) develop and adhere to an effective personal health maintenance program, (4) adopt a healthier lifestyle, and (5) reduce medical care costs by eliminating unnecessary visits to doctors and hospitals.

The corporate objectives for Taking Care that were communicated to department facilitators emphasize its anticipated positive impact on the bottom line to a greater extent. These include: (1) reduce the health costs of both employees and the company, (2) create a healthier work force, (3) improve knowledge and behaviors that affect health habits and medical care choices, (4) create a supportive health environment for employees and their families, (5) increase productivity at work and at home by learning new self-care skills, having healthier bodies, and feeling and looking better, (6) provide employees with the infor-

Table 3.3
Stages in the Fitness Program Innovation Process

STAGE	DATE	MAJOR ACTIVITIES
I. INITIATION:		
1. AGENDA-SETTING	1970s-1980s:	Health care costs escalate, reducing VIC's profits.
2. MATCHING	1978:	VIC establishes an internal team to investigate new products for group insurance customers.
	1980:	Team develops and sells a number of new products to customers under the name Contain.
	1982:	Contain committee established to determine which products to market internally, and how to measure the products' impact on employees' behavior.

- - - - - - - - - - - - - - - The Decision to Adopt- - - - - - - - - - - - - - - -

STAGE	DATE	MAJOR ACTIVITIES
	8/82:	Chairman approves committee's proposal to implement Contain products internally and measure their effects, at an estimated cost of $1,000,000/year.
II. IMPLEMENTATION:		
3. REDEFINING/ RESTRUCTURING	8/82:	Increased employee cost-sharing of health care benefits begins.
	1982:	VIC buys half the shares of the Center for Corporate Fitness & Health Care Promotion.
	1983:	Taking Care products marketed to employees.
	1/84:	Second increase in the level of employee cost-sharing of health care benefits begins. Second opinion program for surgery started.
	7/85:	Corporate Taking Care director hired. Construction of $3 million dollar fitness center proposed and approved.
4. CLARIFYING	3/86:	Evaluation program started to track benefits use by employees.
	4/86:	Quarterly analysis of baseline group begins.
	9/85:	Taking Care facilitators attend corporate training session.

Table 3.3 (continued)

STAGE	DATE	MAJOR ACTIVITIES
	1/86:	Top management approves department working committees. Focus activities begin.
	6/86:	Fitness center "dog and pony" shows are held throughout VIC.
	10/86:	Fitness center opens at headquarters.
5. ROUTINIZING	1987:	Three mini-fitness centers scheduled to open at VIC locations in the field.

mation needed to make appropriate and intelligent health care decisions, and (7) promote VIC as a leader in health care cost containment.

The director has also trained departmental facilitators to lead focus group activities starting in January 1986. Although the newsletters had been sent out for a number of years, the focus activities didn't occur until after the full-time director came on board. Supported by working committees with employee members who were approved by top department management, the focus activities topic varies each quarter. For 1986 the topics were: smoking, weight control, stress management, and exercise. Focus activities usually include: tent cards in the employee cafeteria, videos, and group meetings and contests that each department tailors to their local population. In Data Processing, a popular activity was a contest to walk 5600 miles in lunchtime walking groups that were led by a division vice president. In Financial Services, scales were placed on every floor by the snack machines. Buttons, yardsticks, and prizes were distributed to sanction a weight loss contest between floors, which had the slogan, "A pound of flesh for FS."

Despite the local creativity of these focus activities, interviews with the department facilitators yielded a number of implementation problems. Of major concern was the lack of corporate money to support any of the participation efforts. Although all printed materials are provided by the Corporate Personnel department, the facilitators felt they shouldn't have had to scramble for local funds to sponsor the contests. Perhaps the real issue is that the Taking Care program has not gotten the necessary level of local ownership to obtain the departmental approval of a few hundred dollars to support focus activities. As a 1986 memo by the Financial Services Taking Care facilitator bemoaned, "This program does not have much of a priority with senior management." The facilitator's memo then asks the Taking Care director to send a memo to the marketing group senior vice president to request additional financial support.

Besides money, other implementation problems have surfaced. Not all employees have received the focus materials. There is wide variance between departments in the activeness of focus groups. Also, some of the working committee members weren't really volunteers—a few told me that they felt pressured to join the committees because management had heard they were jocks, but their hearts aren't into leading Taking Care focus efforts. In addition, initial evaluation research shows that only 17% of employees are aware that employee working committees even exist, and only about a third of all employees have participated in at least one focus activity. The Taking Care director commented on these results, "It's my opinion that perhaps the selection of individuals from personnel as facilitators wasn't the best way to mainstream the program."

FLEXTIME

In September 1983 the senior vice president of Corporate Personnel sent a memo to the chairman requesting approval of a proposal to introduce flextime into headquarters, despite VIC's dismal history of experimentation with flexible working hours. In 1974 it had adopted a staggered hours work program for 18 months. The staggered hours program was not a success, as it resulted in a loss of supervisory control of the workforce and a feeling on the part of VIC supervisors that the company suffered a substantial loss of productivity. However, in the intervening years, a number of changes had taken place in society, which caused VIC management to rethink their position on work schedules. These changes included a broadening of legal rights of employees in their relationship with their employer, an increasing emphasis on dignity of the individual in the workplace, the growing number of working mothers, and increasing recognition of the rights of employees to participate in decisions affecting their working lives.

The company also had an equally important practical reason for making the change to flextime: traffic. VIC's offices were located in a major downtown urban area, which was expanding dramatically with the working population expected to increase by 28,500 by 1990. The public transportation system was virtually at capacity during rush hours. It was expected only to get worse as major highway and street construction was underway on most of the surrounding roads and planned new building openings would bring more people downtown.

The memo contended that the introduction of flextime would easily accompany other changes: the opening of new office buildings and a proposed increase in the lunch period from 45 minutes to an hour. Two weeks later, the chairman wrote back:

I support this and see it as an opportunity to increase productivity. Maybe Quality Circles can be used in conjunction with this. For instance, if we were to phase this in with Q.C. dialogue, lots of people could address productivity needs . . . I also see our new buildings and related moves as morale and work climate opportunities—not just hours and job focus but: 1. Dress code, 2. Cleanliness around space, 3. Team spirit kinds of relationships. I hope our corporate and department people will really think about cultural impact here.

Although relating flextime to other innovations that were being adopted may have been on the chairman's mind, the HR management never mentioned quality circles during the implementation of flextime. Perhaps this is because flextime had corporate ownership, whereas quality circles had departmental ownership.

Table 3.4 summarizes key events in the innovation process for flextime. The initiation stage lasted about two years before the chairman approved adoption. A task force of high level personnel representatives was formed in September 1981 to examine the kind of flexible working hours to adopt, in light of the commuting problems expected to ensue from the deteriorating public transportation system and increasing congestion in the downtown area.

Concurrent with the task force's work, a corporate personnel director piloted staggered hours in two field offices over a four-month period. The pilot was deemed a success, as a survey found that about two-thirds of responding supervisors felt staggered hours had no negative impact on productivity. The difference between staggered hours and flextime is that flextime allows greater individual flexibility. A staggered hours program allows employees to choose from several fixed starting times developed around an arrival band of hours, a core band where all employees are at work, and a departure band. Under staggered hours, an employee must arrive on or before his or her chosen start time. In contrast, under flextime an employee may start work at anytime during the morning arrival band and quitting time is determined by when he or she started work that day.

Based on the success of the pilot project, in February 1983, the task force requested the corporate personnel director to develop a staggered hours proposal to be shelved until it was needed. Subsequently, the task force disbanded and over the next year, the director quietly continued his research on flexible working hours. He developed an elaborate flextime proposal, which in his words, ultimately ''sailed through'' the chairman's office.

In December 1983, the flextime innovator's boss, the senior vice president of personnel, sent a memo with a copy of the chairman's approval note to all line management in headquarters. His memo listed a variety of embellished goals for introducing flextime: the reduction of problems resulting from increased traffic and highway construction, the signaling to employees VIC's belief that they are capable of participating in decisions affecting their jobs, an expected increase in productivity, an enhanced ability to attract employees at all levels, and the supporting of downtown merchants by adopting a lengthened lunch period, which would facilitate noontime shopping.

By January 1984, Corporate Personnel invited representatives from all human resource departments to a meeting to introduce flextime and solicit their ideas. The draftsman of the flextime proposal led the meeting and recalled: ''You've got to get them (the Human Resources department representatives) to buy into it. If they come out of the meeting thinking it's their idea—fine! You've got to sell it.'' One of the main clarifying issues to be resolved at the meetings was how to determine which employee groups, if any, were to be excluded from

Table 3.4
Stages in the Flextime Innovation Process

STAGE	DATE	MAJOR ACTIVITIES
I. INITIATION:		
1. AGENDA-SETTING	6/75:	VIC ends staggered hours program after 18 month experiment.
	1978:	Local leading competitor adopts flextime.
	1975-	
	1983:	Traffic congestion and major highway construction around VIC increases dramatically.
2. MATCHING	9/81:	Task force on flexible hours established.
	1981-	
	1982:	Four month experiments with staggered hours conducted at two field offices.
	2/82:	Task force asks member of Corporate Personnel to develop and shelve staggered hours proposal.
	9/83:	Flextime proposal developed and sent to Chairman.

- - - - - - - - - - - - - - - The Decision to Adopt- - - - - - - - - - - - - - -

	10/83:	Proposal "sails through" the Chairman's office.
II. IMPLEMENTATION:		
3. REDEFINING/ RESTRUCTURING	12/83:	Announcement on flextime sent to officers.
	1/84:	Corporate Personnel meets with department Human Resources representatives.
	2/84:	General announcement on flextime appears in company newspaper.
		Press release on flextime sent to local papers.
		Corporate Personnel holds second meeting with department representatives. A key issue that was discussed was how to determine which employee groups to exclude from flextime.
	3/84:	Training meetings held with supervisors to distribute and review written guides.

Table 3.4 (continued)

STAGE	DATE	MAJOR ACTIVITIES
		Questions on the impact of flextime on security, recordkeeping, vanpool parking, and the cafeteria were raised and answered.
	4/84:	Flextime implemented at headquarters.
	6/84:	City bus companies change schedules.
4. CLARIFYING	6/84:	Financial Services executives survey managers and supervisors on flextime's impact on productivity.
	7/84:	Corporate Personnel holds update meeting with department representatives to clarify questions pertaining to the longer lunch hours and to determine whether efficiency has decreased.
5. ROUTINIZING	7/84:	Corporate Personnel determines the amount of time that records of employee time sheets need to be retained.

flextime. (Ultimately, employees in the printshop and the data center were exempt due to "business necessity." Subsequently, a quality circle in the data center chose to study the feasibility of introducing flextime as its first problem, which was ultimately rejected after their presentation to management.)

In February the first general employee announcement of the innovation appeared in the company newspaper. The article chimed:

It appears that flextime . . . might properly be subtitled "Everybody Wins—Nobody Loses." [Employees] win in that they will have the opportunity to better integrate their working day with the demands of their private lives. The City . . . wins in that there should be . . . less . . . traffic. . . . Merchants win because the longer lunch . . . allows for more shopping. . . . And VIC wins because other employers with similar programs have experienced improved productivity as employees assume greater responsibility toward their work.

A news release was also sent to the city newspaper, which countered with a lead editorial applauding VIC for introducing flextime.

A second meeting on implementing flextime was held in March with the departmental personnel representatives. Supervisory guides on how to manage flextime were distributed and publicity was given to the upcoming supervisor training meetings. The purpose of the supervisor training sessions was to explain their role in managing flextime: (1) to communicate it to employees, (2) to administer the sign-in/sign-out time sheets, and (3) to monitor the work schedule to ensure office coverage. Questions were raised and answered regarding flextime's impact on a number of administrative features of the human resource management system: time-keeping (record sheets were now being introduced for *all* employees, not just hourly ones), vanpool scheduling, security, parking, and the cafeteria.

Two weeks before the implementation date, the local bus companies changed their schedules to accommodate flextime. At the end of April, flextime was introduced to over 10,000 VIC employees with virtually no major problems. As a human resources director in Data Processing recalled: "A lot of the problems we had anticipated didn't develop as problems." In June a large division of the Financial Services department with a lot of clerical workers sent a survey to its officers and managers on the effects of flextime on productivity. Results from the survey suggested that management felt flextime had not negatively affected productivity. Many comments were also made regarding flextime's positive impact on morale.

Corporate Personnel conducted its own follow-up session with the department human resources representatives and concluded that overall impressions of flextime were "positive." It appears that 85% of all employees were opting to start work at the beginning of the startup band: 7:00 A.M. and leave at 3:30 P.M. A number of representatives commented, "It's amazing. People who could never get to work by 7:45 before flextime now sign-in at 7 A.M. every day. Tardiness has been virtually eliminated." Many of the representatives also felt efficiency had not decreased and may have increased; however, no plans were made to empirically measure the impact of flextime on productivity.

A single negative issue surfaced at the meeting: "Only the expanded lunch period received comment as a change not welcomed by all employees." Some employees resented the fact that they were not surveyed before the decision was made to adopt the hour-long lunch, particularly since it extended the work day by 15 minutes. They felt that either the hour lunch should be rescinded or employees should be given a choice on the length of their lunches. Other employees felt that the additional 15-minute lunch period was not adopted to serve the interest of employees, but rather to both bolster downtown merchants' sales and support upper management's perceptions of it as a means of stopping extended lunch abuses. However, the negative reaction by this minority group of workers had no impact on implementation. By July 1984, flextime was becoming routinized, as the chief remaining clarifying issue was, "How long do flextime timesheets need to be retained by law?"

FLEXIBLE BENEFITS

When a human resources director was queried about the Flexible Spending Account, he answered, "I can't talk to you much on that. That was handled totally on a corporate basis. We showed films and provided contact names. We had zero questions. For some reason, people didn't get excited about it." His comment epitomizes the history of flexible benefits, an option added to VIC's benefits program in the spring of 1986, which is shown in Table 3.5.

Table 3.5
Stages in the Flexible Benefits Innovation Process

STAGE	DATE	MAJOR ACTIVITIES
I. INITIATION:		
1. AGENDA-SETTING	1970s- 1980s:	Health care costs escalate, reducing VIC's profits.
		Major leading competitors experiment with flexible benefits.
		Employees habitually write suggestions on the on-going opinion survey that implore management to give greater assistance with day care, vision, and hearing expenses.
2. MATCHING	1984:	Chairman of Contain committee sponsors study of flexible benefits. Consultant hired.

- - - - - - - - - - - - - - - The Decision to Adopt- - - - - - - - - - - - - -

STAGE	DATE	MAJOR ACTIVITIES
	3/85:	Contain committee approves flexible benefits "in concept" and authorized the design of a plan.
II. IMPLEMENTATION:		
3. REDEFINING/ RESTRUCTURING	3/85:	Committee wrestles with design issue of whether existing benefits should be included in plan, which would cost a lot more than including new benefits.
	3/85:	Computer system to support the operation of flexible benefits begins to be designed and built.
	10/85:	Officers sent announcement concerning the plan to adopt flexible benefits.
	3/86:	General announcement of flexible benefits appears in company newspaper.
	4/86:	Flyers sent to employees' homes.
	5/86:	Packets sent to employees' homes.
	6/86:	Employee sign-up period begins
	7/86:	Program formally begins.
4. CLARIFYING	7/86:	Key clarification issue arises: the lack of employee response to innovation.
5. ROUTINIZING		

The purpose of the Flexible Spending Account is to allow employees to save on taxes by paying for certain health care expenses not covered by the company insurance plan, such as vision, hearing, and dependent care expenses, with before-tax salary. The Flexible Spending Account can be viewed as a basic form of cafeteria benefits, which is a program that allows employees a choice in the design of their benefits packages. According to a corporate director, "the Flexible Spending Account is a vanilla cafeteria benefits plan that covers a few areas to start with and we could always add more." The Flexible Spending Account brochure lists its formal employee objectives: to *save* automatically for expenses, to *reduce taxes* by allowing less salary subject to taxation, and to *increase disposable income*. As the personnel director's comment eluded, these reasons were not compelling enough to generate much employee enthusiasm.

When asked why VIC adopted the Flexible Spending Account, the director said, "Where the rubber meets the road, we were after employee day care needs. We heard there was a crying need for day care assistance and we simply weren't willing to build day care centers." Other human resource professionals saw a different agenda and viewed the Flexible Spending Account as part of a total company strategy of health care cost containment. FSA was seen as a significant intervention to take an aggressive approach to help VIC reshape the whole design of the benefits system. Whereas many companies are fat, dumb, and happy and locked into future health care costs, FSA was a means of jumping on the corporate cafeteria benefits bandwagon in a way that provided tax advantages for both the company and employees. Unfortunately, some executives blame the 1986 change in the federal tax regulations as a prime factor contributing to the poor employee response to FSA. As one executive said, "Prior to the regulatory changes, if people didn't use the money set aside they could keep it and put it into savings. Now the new regulations state that employees lose what they don't spend. Also, it is difficult to communicate a choice program to employees, because it's threatening to them. We wanted to start with a relatively simple program that we can add more choices to through the years. Even though it's a plain vanilla plan, employees are petrified of this."

When asked why the company didn't adopt a full-scale cafeteria benefits plan that was integrated with the existing employee insurance plan, one HR executive explained VIC's approach to human resources management innovation in this way: "We wanted to move very slowly as we went along. We're like IBM in many respects. We want to view what other competitors are doing and get empirical evidence and then improve upon it incrementally. It doesn't bother us to be second or third. By incremental improvements you become leading edge. You might lag a bit on the Flexible Spending Account and then make a flashy showboat thrust all at once." The executive pointed out that the American Can Corporation, an early innovator, had spent millions on cafeteria benefits. By waiting to adopt flexible benefits, VIC's strategy was to learn from early innovators' mistakes and investment. In 1984 the Contain committee hired a leading benefits consulting firm to design a program. It offered a full-scale cafeteria benefits plan, which in the words of the vice president was "really nifty." Although some executives would have loved to have put it in at VIC, the company wasn't ready for it. Rather, VIC executives were looking for a first step and saw the Flexible Spending Account as a trial balloon to float.

Under the tutelage of its chair, the Contain committee approved the Flexible Spending Account "in concept" in the spring of 1985 with a target start date of January 1986. According to the account director, the biggest restructuring issue was determining whether benefits currently covered by the company plan should be part of the Flexible Spending Account. Since it has not been proven that cafeteria benefits result in reduced insurance costs, he believes members of the Contain committee backed off from adopting a full-scale plan, because they felt that adoption without more evidence would run counter to their cost containment stance.

Once this restructuring issue was resolved, a computer system had to be designed to automatically deduct dollars for the Flexible Spending Account from an employee's paycheck. Because the system was finished several months behind schedule, the start date was pushed back to July 1986. In total, the Flexible Spending Account costs about a half a million dollars to build the computer system, $150,000 to develop employee promotional materials, and $200,000 per year to operate.

The communication effort for the Flexible Spending Account had a number of tactics. A management announcement was sent out in October 1985. In March 1986, an article announcing the program to all employees appeared in the company newspaper. In April all employees received a flyer in their paychecks and in May packets of promotional materials were sent to their homes. Videos, posters, and telephone hot lines are examples of additional publicity efforts. The first employee sign-up period was held in May and had to be extended to the end of June because of lack of employee response. Ultimately, only about 400 out of VIC's 30,000 employees signed up to start the program in July. Of this group, only 206 of the 10,000 headquarters employees had subscribed. In a September 1986 interview, the director of the Flexible Spending Account bemoaned, "Now, I wish we'd never put it in; we expected a bigger response. On the attitude surveys, people complained that eye glasses, hearing aids, and cosmetic surgery weren't covered and that the company should do more for day care. The poor response is due to the threat that employees won't get their money back unless they get a bill."

THE CASH AWARDS

When asked why VIC management decided to implement The Outstanding Achievement Awards Program (TOAAP), the senior corporate analyst providing its technical support said, "Because senior personnel management approved it now." Similarly, when given the same question, the analyst's boss, the director of compensation and benefits, said, "Why now? I can't tell you why we put it in now rather than five years ago. It's something we had wanted to do in compensation for a long time. Everyone talks about pay for performance unless they're unionized. Because of the cumbersomeness of a merit salary increase system, now there's less emphasis on salary as a fixed cost—more emphasis on variable compensation. We want incentive compensation moved down to the lower levels of the corporation.''

VIC employees, on the other hand, were given a somewhat less haphazard explanation of the rationale behind adoption in a spring 1986 article in the company. Reporting an interview with the senior vice president of personnel, employees were told that TOAAP was being implemented to provide employees with another means of receiving pay for performance. Whereas merit increases recognize employees' sustained levels of performance, achievement awards are one-time cash payments that reward exceptional contributions when they occur. Except for designated participants in other incentive plans, all full-time salaried employees at all levels are eligible.

In the article the vice president also explained the way the program works. Management nominates employees who they believe have made an outstanding contribution, which significantly enhances the productivity or effectiveness of a business group, by completing a nomination form that outlines the achievement. Obviously, standards will vary, because each department will develop its own specific criteria. Completed forms then go to a department head for review, who then submits the form to a group head for approval. Payroll will process the checks and deliver them for distribution to the group head by the end of the month.

VIC chose a loosely structured innovation design, because it wanted to meet the business needs of each department. Although there are corporate guidelines, it's really administered in each area. The awards should be in the range of a minimum of $250 to a maximum of 15% of an employee's salary, with 80% in the range of 5%. Each department's goal should be to reward 10% of their population in any one year.

As the summary of the history of TOAAP in Table 3.6 shows, the cash award program proposal, which was developed by the director of Corporate Compensation, was formally approved for adoption by senior management in January 1986. Then a key restructuring issue arose: Where would the money come from? In order to build consensus for the awards, the director approached groups of key personnel members of each department to "bounce ideas off critical managers." The departmental representatives felt corporate monies should pay for the program, whereas corporate personnel members thought the departments should pay for it out of their merit increase budgets, which are allocated according to employee population and salary grade distribution. A compromise was finally reached. The Corporate Personnel department would add a 1/20% increase to each merit budget if each department would allocate one-half of 1% of its merit budget to the program. The director felt that the amount of the departmental contributions was not unreasonable, because it "probably would be available anyway through turnover and normal attrition." As one manager who administers the cash awards in the Financial Services department countered in an interview, however, "The kicker was we got to pay for it out of our salary budget. It's kinda like robbing Peter to pay Paul."

Table 3.6
Stages in the Cash Awards Innovation Process

STAGE	DATE	MAJOR ACTIVITIES
I. INITIATION:		
1. AGENDA-SETTING	1980s:	Other Fortune 500 companies increasingly experiment with incentive plans for all levels of employees.
2. MATCHING	1985:	The Director of Corporate Compensation develops a proposal for an incentive plan that pays employees cash bonuses for outstanding performance.
- - - - - - - - - - - - - - The Decision to Adopt- - - - - - - - - - - - - - -		
II. IMPLEMENTATION:	1/86:	A senior vice president approves the proposal.
3. REDEFINING/ RESTRUCTURING	Spring 1986:	The director surveys representatives from each human resource departments to see if they would fund the program using their existing merit budgets.
	3/86:	Corporate Personnel and the departments reach a compromise on funding the awards: an extra one half of one percent will be allocated to the budgets if the money will be used for the awards. Program announced to officers and managers.
	4/86:	Program described in article in company newspaper. Outstanding Achievement Award committees formed in each department.
	5/86:	Program officially begins.
4. CLARIFYING	6/86:	Payroll has problems with processing the awards. Line management in some depart ments, such as Financial Services, is slow to start program. Many managers ask for clarific- ation on what constitutes an "outstanding achievement".
	8/86:	Financial Services has given 19 awards to 2% of its population over the past 3 months. Data Processing has given 106 awards to 5% of its population over the past 5 months.

In March 1986, a formal announcement was sent from the senior vice president to all management personnel. In April an article appeared in the newspaper to explain the program to all employees, which was when the program officially started. From the corporate director's perspective, the only implementation problem that occurred was "early in the program, we had to beat payroll to deliver the checks immediately." When asked whether all levels of employees received cash awards, the director said, "The first couple of months it didn't filter down much, but the bulk of awards in the last few months (August and September 1986) have been to nonexempt and lower level exempt employees."

A review of the salary levels of employees that have been given awards by Data Processing and Financial Services management, shown in Table 3.7, generally supports this statement. As the chart shows, Data Processing started its program two months earlier than Financial Services did and has given awards to a greater percentage of eligible employees; 5% of the eligible employee population received awards in Data Processing versus 2% in Financial Services. Data Processing has given awards to 106 employees over five months; Financial Services has given 19 awards over three months. On the average, however, Financial Services is more generous than Data Processing in the size of the award. The average amount awarded is $1,474 in Financial Services and $951 in Data Processing.

The reluctance of Financial Services, which is part of the marketing group, to initially jump on the corporate bandwagon is illustrated by excerpts from a June 1986 memo sent by senior management to all vice presidents in the field. "We applaud the corporation's efforts to provide pay-for-performance—in general and as embodied in the concept of this new program for folks who are not otherwise eligible for incentive awards. *It is distressing*, however, that this new program is being introduced at the same time we are struggling to develop, fund, and introduce programs that provide on-going incentive opportunities for people who have accepted key positions in the field. For that reason, *special guidelines* will apply to The Outstanding Achievement Awards Program as it is implemented in the Marketing group in 1986. The bottom line is simple, our priority is to formulate and fund incentive programs for our *key* field positions, but we will also participate in the Outstanding Achievement Awards program."

The special guidelines, in essence, gave a quota of number of awards and total dollars to allocate in each region, which was about one-*quarter* of 1% of the merit budgets. Although he thought the program was a great idea, the vice president of human resources who oversaw its administration in the marketing group couldn't understand the mixed reception his formal presentation on TOAAP had received from the senior staff. He recalled that one executive (who wrote the special guidelines memo) said, "We're not going to do it. We've had the most reorganization in my area and the reorganization has cost a lot of money. There's no money for the Outstanding Achievement Awards in my area." As a result of the lukewarm response from this key executive and others, the marketing group took a conservative approach for 1986. No money was formally budgeted for the program. Publicity was minimized, as the personnel executive made an agreement with the senior staff to not identify departments and not publish names through the group human resources area. The decision to publicize names of recipients was left up to individual departments.

Perhaps this lack of initial top management support is the chief reason why the Awards committee for the Small Accounts Marketing group, which consists of two human resource vice presidents, had not (as of October 1987) developed specific guidelines that define an "outstanding achievement." As one of the committee members explained, "I wanted to get a line management committee to review the awards, but the top executive of the marketing group said a four letter word and we have too many committees. There aren't going to be any more committees." Once the effects of the reorganization settle a little more, however, the program may receive more active line management support.

Data Processing has taken a different approach to publicity and the development of award criteria than marketing. A monthly awards ceremony is held to allow recipients the occasion to shake hands with the top executive in Data Processing in the presence of management. The four person review committee, comprised of three members of the Human Resources division and an assistant to the top executive, also made a few suggestions on how to increase publicity. Individual and group pictures of recipients shaking hands with the top departmental executive will be taken and posted on company bulletin boards. In addition, a recognition letter will be sent to recipients, which will also be posted around the office.

Data Processing has developed five criteria to define outstanding achievements. They are: (1) expected results of assignments are significantly exceeded, (2) extensive extra effort and sacrifice of personal time, (3) ideas are proposed and products are produced that significantly affect productivity, (4) significant improvements are made in work processes, (5) or outstanding ability is demonstrated in responding to emergency situations. In addition, Data Processing has developed special criteria that allow its training staff to reward outstanding students in a class for entry level professional employees. Recipients must consistently perform above average in academic areas and "show a clear commitment to VIC Data Processing values," which may be shown by such behavior as helping other students. In contrast to Financial Services, Data Processing resists applying a quota approach to its guidelines: "There are no specific quota of awards to be given each month."

Despite Data Processing's written guidelines, key clarifying issues still remain regarding the criteria for outstanding achievements. As one Data Processing personnel director notes, "The danger of a program like this is making sure we use the right criteria. We should not give Joe an award for doing a good job for a long time or the program will lose credibility and go down the tubes. One of the difficulties in Data Processing is we use a team approach and sometimes it's difficult to identify individual contributions . . . However, senior management has responded very favorably to it. It's a super program. Anytime you do something like this, you run the risk of annoying people who don't get it. But more is gained than lost as long as we don't reward longevity. Also, one of the things people forget is there is a limited amount of money to reward people."

As this comment alludes, half a year after its inception the Data Processing

Table 3.7

Number and Amount of Achievement Awards Given to Each Salary Level Group by Department

MONTH	Manager & Officer		Professional		Nonexempt		Total	
	Number	Dollars	Number	Dollars	Number	Dollars	Number	Dollars
April Data Processing	1	(1000)	1	(2500)			13	(13,750)
			2	(1500)				
			1	(1250)				
			3	(1000)				
			2	(750)			April average: 1058	
			3	(500)				
May Data Processing			3	(3500)			24	(28,500)
			1	(2500)				
			1	(2000)				
			5	(1000)				
			6	(750)				
			6	(500)	2	(500)	May average: 1188	
June Data Processing	1	(500)	4	(1500)			24	(19,000)
			3	(1000)				
			3	(750)				
			6	(500)				
			5	(250)			June average: 792	
Financial Services	1	(2000)	3	(2000)	2	(1000)	9	(13,000)
	1	(1000)	1	(1500)	1	(500)	June average: 1444	
July								
Data Processing			1	(2000)	1	(500)	26	(21,650)
			2	(1500)				
	1	(1200)	1	(1200)				
			8	(1000)				
			1	(750)				
	1	(500)	9	(500)				
			2	(250)			July average: 833	
Financial Services			1	(2000)	1	(1000)		
			1	(1500)	1	(750)		
			1	(1250)			6	(7,500)
			1	(1000)			July average: 1250	

Table 3.7 (continued)

MONTH	Manager & Officer		Professional		Nonexempt		Total	
	Number	Dollars	Number	Dollars	Number	Dollars	Number	Dollars
August								
Data Processing	1	(1500)	1	(2000)			19	(17,950)
			1	(1200)				
			10	(1000)			August average: 945	
			1	(750)				
			5	(500)				
Financial Services	1	(2000)	1	(2500)	1	(2000)	4	(7,500)
			1	(1000)			August average: 1900	

Financial Services has given 19 awards totaling $28,000 to 2% of its employees, with an average award of $1,474. Data Processing has given 106 awards totaling $100,850 to 5% of its employees, with an average of $951.

committee was faced with trying to manage growing demand for the innovation. According to the top executive's assistant, the chief bookkeeper of TOAAP, August 1986 was the first month where Data Processing had major turndowns. Out of 38 nominees, 19 were turned down. Some of the rejections were group awards that the senior vice president wouldn't sign off on, since awards are supposed to recognize individual accomplishments. In other cases, nominators were asked to reconsider the amount of the award. Some awards were turned down for not having enough information, and others because they involved achievement in educational development and not a work achievement. As the bookkeeper stated, "Although over time we want to cover 25% (far greater than corporate guidelines suggest) of the home office staff . . . if we didn't approach this in a disciplined and organized fashion, if we went about it half-cocked, we'd be in trouble."

THE PEER RECOGNITION PROGRAM

Perhaps one reason members of senior marketing management weren't initially more receptive to TOAAP is because it competed with an established home-grown innovation: The People Are Tops (PAT) employee recognition program. When its administrator was asked why it was introduced, he said, "I got the assignment from my boss. I'm not sure where he got it from, but I think he read about it in the library." Indeed, a review of the recognition program's file yielded articles with such titles as "The Psychology of Noncash Incentives" and "Motivation: Noncash Awards Bring Out the Little Extra in Everyone," as well as materials describing other insurance companies' recognition programs. The latter were solicited by the members of a 1983 task force, which was led by the soon-

Table 3.8
Stages in the Peer Recognition Innovation Process

STAGE	DATE	MAJOR ACTIVITIES
I. <u>INITIATION</u>:		
1. AGENDA-SETTING	1983:	Director reads about employee recognition programs in library.
	5/83:	Interdivisional task force established to develop recognition program for long-term employees.
	12/83:	Implementation of recognition program included in 1984 goals for the Financial Services Human Resources Department.
2. MATCHING	2/85:	Task force presents proposal to senior line management.
- - - - - - - - - - - - - - - - The Decision to Adopt- - - - - - - - - - - - - -		
	2/85:	Senior management of Financial Services approves proposal.
	3/85:	Corporate Personnel approves Financial Services proposal.
II. <u>IMPLEMENTATION</u>:		
3. REDEFINING/ RESTRUCTURING	3/85:	Employee Recognition Committee formed. Division heads nominate representatives for the People Are Tops divisional committees.
4. CLARIFYING	6/85:	People Are Tops kick-off held. Some employees complain that the review process is too bureaucratic. Some employees want clarification on the difference between a People Are Tops and a Spot award.
	10/85:	First $500 Quarterly Award given.
	1/86:	Perfect Attendance Award started.
	4/86:	Mystery Employee Contest held.
5. ROUTINIZING	6/86:	Rotation of Employee Recognition Committee members begins.
		Corporate edict given that the Outstanding Achievement Awards supercede all other cash award programs.

Table 3.8 (continued)

STAGE	DATE	MAJOR ACTIVITIES
	7/86:	Marketing Group Human Resources plans to diffuse People Are Tops Award to all departments.
	9/86:	Meeting held with employees to "Reintroduce People Are Tops".

to-be named administrator of the PAT program, the manager of quality circles in Financial Services.

As Table 3.8 shows, at the end of 1983, the task force's proposal for an employee recognition program was favorably reviewed by the top human resource executive and its implementation was placed in the 1984 human resource business plans. A meeting was scheduled with the senior line managers in Financial Services in February to get their approval. The People Are Tops program was marketed as another way to help create a positive image of the department by providing recognition for employees in the lower echelons who put extra effort into their jobs. A task force member explained, "What we are trying to do is to reward people who are solid citizens, who aren't superstars, but who come to work everyday and do their jobs well." The formal objectives of the PAT program listed in the proposal were: to foster quality work and outstanding personal service by each employee, to motivate all employees to apply their best effort in performing their jobs, to emphasize and communicate to employees the importance of each individual as a contributor to the success of the entire department's operation, and to build employee pride in the organization and willingness to go the extra mile. Except for a minor question on the tax implications of the program (the awards are taxable), the program was approved by line management and was off and running.

The award is open to all employees except officers; a nomination may be made by anyone regardless of title or position. Nominees must demonstrate outstanding contributions in at least two of the following seven categories: attitude, self-development, productivity, business knowledge, contribution to the organization, working with others, and leadership. Using many of the individuals who had served on personnel advisory committees in the past, an employee recognition committee was organized to oversee the program. Divisional committees that are subordinate to the employee recognition committee were composed using representatives from various salary levels. The divisional committees review nominations and coordinate the giving of the awards. The chairpersons of the divisional committees also serve on the employee recognition committee.

A recipient is notified of his selection by his divisional committee. The winner receives a small gift, such as, a SONY walkman or dinner for two at a local restaurant. If a winner chooses to accept the award, a ceremony is held in her work area where the division head hands the award to her in front of her co-workers. A snapshot of the ceremony with a description of the award winner's favorable qualities is placed on her floor. Every quarter one individual is selected from the past group of recipients to receive a $500 cash award.

Another feature of the program is the SPOT awards, which refers not to an acronym but rather to the concept of giving an employee recognition "on the spot" for doing a good job. A SPOT award, which is a tote bag with a Financial Services logo on it, is distributed by senior line managers to any nonofficer they believe has made an outstanding contribution to the organization in a job, position, or on a special assignment. Employee interviews and questionnaire results indicated that most employees do not understand the difference between the SPOT and PAT awards.

Formal approval for the PAT program was obtained from the Corporate Personnel department in March 1985. By June the program was officially announced in a memo to Financial Services management as an employee Recognition Program award, which is intended to reward and acknowledge exceptional performance of all *nonofficer* employees. It is interesting to note that no mention of the innovation's original intent, the recognition for long-term employees who are solid citizens, was made in this official announcement.

Concurrent with the announcement, a wide range of publicity activities was conducted. Posters were placed on each floor's bulletin boards. Brochures were distributed and flipcharts with pictures of members of the divisional committees and the merchandise were put up. Boxes filled with nomination forms were prominently placed in the vending areas, and key rings and note pads were passed out by a gorilla during the lunch hour.

Over time, however, as more and more employees were nominated for awards, a key clarifying issue arose regarding the review process. Some employees felt that the committee reviews of the nomination forms and critiques of the ways in which they are written were too stringent. As one employee complained, for example, "I nominated someone for an award and they made me try to quantify her job and results to the point where I wasn't able to give them her shoe size. She wasn't in a job where her outputs were easily measured, yet she was an outstanding contributor." Another employee remarked, "I tried to nominate someone and they decided she only deserved a SPOT award. I think the People Are Tops awards are biased toward people in the Customer Service division." In response to criticisms such as these, committee members offered assistance to any nominator desiring help in writing the nomination form.

In January 1986, the Perfect Attendance award was added to the PAT program. As it sounds, this award honors professional and nonexempt employees who have perfect attendance records. Recipients are invited to have lunch with their officers in the executive dining room.

By April, however, the employee recognition committee had developed the perception that employee enthusiasm for the program was waning. In an effort to generate renewed interest, a mystery employee contest was established. Employees were encouraged to nominate a coworker who they thought might be the mystery person on the basis of clues given by the committee. At the end of

Table 3.9
Number of People Are Tops Awards Given since Inception

<u>THIRD QUARTER 1985 - 54 AWARDS</u>

    1 Quarterly Award
  20 Merchandise Awards
  33 Spot Awards

<u>FOURTH QUARTER - 1985 - 31 AWARDS</u>

    1 Quarterly Award
    9 Merchandise Awards
  21 Spot Awards

<u>FIRST QUARTER 1986 - 125 AWARDS</u>

      1 Quarterly Award
      9 Merchandise Awards
      7 Spot Awards
  108 Perfect Attendance Awards

<u>SECOND QUARTER 1986 - 44 AWARDS</u>

   0 Quarterly Awards*
  11 Merchandise Awards
   7 Spot Awards
  26 Perfect Attendance Awards

*Replaced by Outstanding Achievement Awards

the contest, a lottery was held where 26 of the names of the employees entered in the contest were drawn out of a hat to receive a merchandise award. One of the original task members disagreed with the whole idea of a contest, which he did not view as being a professional means of promoting PAT participation. He felt that the effort "seems more like fun and games. The contest does not generate . . . submissions; it is only another lottery."

In June 1986, the program had been in existence for a year and members of the committee started to rotate as the innovation became more routinized. As Table 3.9 shows, a total of 254 awards had been given for all categories. During June the quarterly cash award was eliminated due to a corporate edict that all cash awards with the exception of the Management Incentive Plan are now superseded by the Outstanding Achievement Award program. This latter action exemplifies some of the politics of human resource innovation: a corporate-sponsored innovation can sometimes "pull rank" on a departmental one.

Despite the advent of the Outstanding Achievement Award program, in June the human resources vice president of the marketing group approved the diffusion of the PAT award to the rest of the group, "since it's a proven product and doesn't cost a lot of money." To prepare for the implementation of the program throughout the unit, the innovation was revisited by the employee recognition committee during the fall of 1986 and such questions as, "What is the difference between a People Are Tops and a SPOT award?" were discussed. Another key clarifying issue, which has not yet been resolved, is how to effectively integrate the PAT program with the Outstanding Achievement Award program, which has more employee clout since it involves money. Because the PAT coordinator had sensed that "the program was losing momentum" in Financial Services, separate meetings were held with executives and employees in September to "reintroduce People Are Tops."

EMPLOYEE NEWSLETTER

When the initiator of the Financial Services employee-run newsletter, the *Grapevine*, was asked the reasons for its adoption, he said that low department results for the 1983 corporate opinion survey had provided the main impetus. As Table 3.10 shows, a 1984 goal was established for the Human Resource division "to improve communication among our people," which was prompted by the survey ratings.

The newly appointed editor of the *Grapevine* followed up on this goal with a memo to the divisional vice presidents in April 1984, which stated that one method of accomplishing the goal is to expand the role and usage of the *Personnel Bulletin*. The editor explained that the central theme underlying this effort would be to "toot our own horn and rekindle enthusiasm about being on the Financial Services team." He asked the executives to identify individuals in their respective divisions that could be contacted on a regular basis to write up and submit information that would be beneficial for all Financial Services people to know.

With this handpicked team, the manager of Innovation Through Involvement, People Are Tops, and now the *Grapevine* kicked off the first meeting of the Communications committee in June by stating, "The purpose of the committee is to revise the *Bulletin* and make it more representative of all of Financial Services and publish information that reflects a positive image of the department. We want to make people feel good about being members of the unit." The committee members' names were publicized in the May *Bulletin* to encourage employees to contact members and make suggestions on how to improve the newsletter. Armed with this input, the committee met for an hour a week for several weeks to plan the new publication. Key issues relating to management support for the innovation are found in these minutes from the June 26, 1984 meeting:

Most of the discussion focused on the central issue of getting clarification from senior management on whether the *Bulletin* is seen as a "frill/nice to have" or a serious means of communication for the department. If (it) is seen as a "frill/nice to have" then the consensus . . . was that a quality publication could not be put together in the limited amount of time (one hour per week) that they could devote to it and still avoid slippage in their other work commitments. However, the group did feel that it could make some moderate improvements even with their limited availability. On the other hand, if the *Bulletin* is seen as a serious communications vehicle, adequate time and resources must be devoted to it. The committee's recommendation calls for (1) management support from the top via a memo from the senior vice president and a follow-up memo from the division heads, (2) solicitation of human resources within the department and making this assignment part of that person's responsibilities, and (3) an adequate budget commitment to cover expenses.

The senior vice president of Financial Services was asked to write a cover article for the inaugural issue, and he agreed to do so. The committee decided to adopt a new name for the publication, the *Grapevine*, which was suggested by the underwriting representative, and also develop new features. Additionally, the committee gathered information on the experiences of VIC departments with employee newsletters.

Although not initially apparent from these preliminary meetings, the *Grapevine* was a major innovation in the area of employee communication at VIC. Unlike previous employee newsletters, the *Grapevine* was written using grass-roots employee participation and was basically uncensored. The innovativeness of the newsletter may have occurred as a result of permeation from another innovation, the quality circle program, and the management style of the editor who was also the quality circle program's coordinator.

The first issue of the bimonthly publication came out in September 1984 and showed a dramatic departure in content from that of the *Bulletin*. Whereas the *Bulletin* included items on the objectives of performance appraisals and a field office's new mailing address, the *Grapevine* led with a cover article from the senior executive of Financial Services, which invited employees to suggest items to include in future issues. In addition, recognition was given to employees who participated in such work activities as a successful quality circle presentation or extracurricular ones like a local tennis tournament. There was also a humorous article by Omont, a fictional employee who poked fun at the slowness of the new, talking, "state-of-the-art" elevators, and a feature on the responsibilities of a newly formed work area.

In the next issue, employees were encouraged once again by the top manager to make suggestions regarding the items to include in the newsletter. Employee volunteers were solicited to help work on its staff. The issue also included a point/counterpoint section, which discussed the pros and cons of VIC's new paperless office campaign, and Omont had moved on to the food in the cafeteria. In subsequent issues, introductory articles were written by the top executive's direct reports, and employees wrote such features as a humorous blurb on the top executive being stuck for twelve minutes in one of the new elevators, a story recognizing employees for outside activities like leading a Cambodian refugee support group or coaching Little League, and Letters to the Editor. The regular columns covered somewhat controversial topics. The Omont column questioned the fairness of the performance appraisal process, and point/counterpoint had moved onto flextime and smoking.

Table 3.10
Stages in the Employee Newsletter Innovation Process

STAGE	DATE	MAJOR ACTIVITIES
I. INITIATION:		
1. AGENDA-SETTING	1983:	Opinion survey results indicate employee morale is low.
		1984 goal set to improve communication within Financial Services.
2. MATCHING	1/84:	Director asks subordinate to start editing the Personnel Bulletin.

- - - - - - - - - - - - - - - The Decision to Adopt- - - - - - - - - - - - - -

	3/84:	Director and Editor decide to expand coverage to all divisions and to cover stories outside the realm of Personnel.
II. IMPLEMENTATION:		
3. REDEFINING/ RESTRUCTURING	4/84:	Memo sent to division heads requesting nominations of employees to work on staff. Nominees' names printed in Bulletin. Employees invited to contact nominees to make suggestions on ways to revise the Bulletin.
	5/84:	Nominees begin meeting to define mission, to select a name, and to determine the new features of the newsletter. Members contact other VIC departments to collect information on newsletters.
		Members raise the issue of whether top management is committed to the publication.
	9/84:	First issue of Grapevine appears with a front page commentary written by the top management.
	11/84:	General announcement appears in Grapevine soliciting volunteers to serve on staff.
	1/85:	Heads of divisions start writing articles.
4. CLARIFYING	10/85:	Grapevine surveys readers on their likes and dislikes.
	1/86:	Reorganization of Financial Services.
	3/86:	Grapevine eliminated. Marketing Group Exchange created.

Table 3.10 (continued)

STAGE	DATE	MAJOR ACTIVITIES
	6/86:	Financial Services Senior Executive resurrects <u>Grapevine</u>.
		Employee editor appointed.
	10/86:	First issue since reorganization.
5. ROUTINIZING		

The editorial criticizing the smoking policy was the only article ever censored in the *Grapevine*. Management asked the writer who criticized the lack of enforcement of the existing smoking policy "to tone it down." The original article, for example, insinuated that the main reason why the policy isn't strongly enforced is because a leading cigarette manufacturer is one of VIC's biggest customers.

In October 1985, the innovation was a year old, and a survey was sent to all employees soliciting information on ways to improve the publication. At the same time as the *Grapevine* was becoming more routinized, Data Processing's employee newsletter was being cut from the budget. It wasn't run using participative management and was in the words of its editor, "strictly monitored by senior staff." A director gave his view on the reason for the newsletter's demise. "I was able to save it through one budget-cutting cycle . . . but a newsletter's a visible thing. Sometimes when something's visible, it gets cut, even though it's not a lot of money (about $2,400 per year)."

Although budgetary issues did not lead to the demise of the *Grapevine*, as its printing costs were covered out of the Personnel division's general funds, the reorganization of the marketing group in January 1986 did. As the editor explained in an article in the last issue of the *Grapevine*:

CHANGE. This simple word can create a nightmare, be a pleasant surprise or be welcomed. For many of you, as well as myself, the changes that have occurred in 1986 fit into one or more of these categories . . . These changes will also affect the *Grapevine*, and I regret to say that this is our last publication. It will be replaced by a new *Marketing Group Exchange* that will focus on the entire organization.

According to one executive, the new group vice president of human resources wanted to get rid of the *Grapevine* and have it replaced by the *Exchange*, which would be written by professionals. In his words, it was a case of "not invented here."

By June 1986, however, the new senior line executive of Financial Services resurrected the *Grapevine*. He asked a talented employee who had volunteered to work on the staff since November 1984 to be its new editor, because in the words of the former editor, "My boss didn't want our area associated with it politically, so it won't compete with the *Exchange*." The newly appointed editor enthusiastically greeted former staff at her first organizing meeting with the words, "Hi! In case you haven't heard, the *Grapevine* is about to be reborn, and we've all been elected midwives."

The first issue of the reincarnated paper came out in October 1986 with an introduction by the new senior executive. "It is with great pleasure that I re-inaugurate the *Grapevine*. Subsequent to the restructuring of the marketing group in January, the *Grapevine* was discontinued, largely because of the reassignment of some of the editorial staff, and also the anticipation of a newsletter that would service . . . the marketing group. Many of you, however, expressed disappointment with the discontinuance. Moreover, as the restructuring began to take shape, it became clear that a place still exists for a Financial Services newsletter. The *Grapevine* plays an important role not only in communicating issues from management, but also in communicating between employees and to management."

There were also articles on the reorganization and recent People Are Tops recipients, a rumor mill, and a point/counterpoint article containing many of the sensitive issues on smoking that had been censored seven months earlier.

COMPARISONS BETWEEN INNOVATIONS

Whereas the innovations are perhaps best understood in terms of the descriptive accounts of their adoption in this chapter, it is useful to examine quantitative and categorical data to allow for comparisons of the adoption process across innovations. Key features of the adoption process are summarized in three tables in this section. Table 3.11 summarizes key features of the initiation of innovation for each program: the pressures for initiating adoption, the date of adoption, the initial sponsor, and whether there was prior initiation.

P. J. DiMaggio's and W. W. Powell's[6] framework of institutional isomorphism, explained in the literature review in the first chapter, can be used to analyze the pressures for initiating adoption. Each innovation is classified as being adopted for primarily coercive, normative, or mimetic pressures. Four of the innovations were adopted because of coercive forces, which stem from political pressures and cultural expectations of legitimacy. The other four programs were adopted because of mimetic pressures, which arise when firms model themselves after successful organizations. Whereas normative forces stemming from the professionalization of the human resources function may have played a contributing secondary role, at VIC these forces were not the primary impetus for adoption. However, this situation may be a function of the nature of the personnel department at VIC and does not necessarily apply to the initiation of human resource innovation in other organizations.

Fear of government fines and the possible loss of federal contracts provided the initial impetus for adopting job posting. Coercive external environmental pressures initiated the innovation process for flextime and the fitness program.

Table 3.11
Key Adoption Features: Initiation

INNOVATION	INITIATION PRESSURES	DATE	SPONSORSHIP	PRIOR INITIATION
JOB POSTING	coercive	4/77	headquarters	no
QUALITY CIRCLES	mimetic	11/83	headquarters	yes
FLEXTIME	coercive	4/84	headquarters	yes
NEWSLETTER	coercive	9/84	local	no
PEER RECOGNITION	mimetic	6/85	local	no
FITNESS PROGRAM	coercive	7/85	headquarters	no
CASH AWARDS	mimetic	4/86	headquarters	yes
FLEXIBLE BENEFITS	mimetic	5/86	headquarters	no

Traffic delays are a perennial problem not only for VIC workers but also for other organizations in the same metropolitan area. Additionally, renovation of the main highway arteries into headquarters was scheduled into the next decade. VIC's management was left with the option of either adopting flexible hours, which would be warmly received by the local political and business community, or putting up with an increasing number of tardy employees and receiving no favorable publicity for helping to ameliorate an urban problem.

As for the fitness program, increasing health care costs were recognized as the main strategic industrial threat to future profitability. If VIC was going to be viewed as a legitimate leader in the management of health care costs, it had to develop proven products in this area. The *Grapevine* was started because of negative internal forces, which could eventually hurt VIC's external image as "being a good place to work." Financial Services had extremely low opinion survey results compared with other VIC divisions, and *something* had to be done to improve employee morale.

Quality circles, the fitness program, the cash awards, and the recognition program were adopted mainly because of the desire of VIC management to copy leading firms or follow the advice given by leading management gurus. Like many Fortune 500 companies in the 1980s, VIC management caught the participative management bug. Many of its leading competitors had introduced quality circles, and VIC did not want to be viewed as being "behind the times." Similarly, flexible benefits were started because many leading companies had introduced flexible benefits and "we wanted to get started in this area." For decades, cash awards have been in vogue in the human resources texts and have caught renewed favor in light of the current increasing competitiveness of many industrial markets in the United States. Coercive pressures were contributing forces to the adoption of cash awards. In these competitive economic times, it is essential to insure that the employees who contribute the most to the organization are paid the most. As for the peer recognition program, books like *In Search of Excellence* and *Theory Z* subtly and not so subtly encourage companies to copy leading firm practices of publicly giving recognition for good performance.

As the sponsorship column of Table 3.11 shows, the headquarters Personnel department plays a critical role in initiating innovation at VIC. Six of the eight innovations were started at the corporate level. Only the two innovations that adopted only in Financial Services were initiated at the local level. A possible explanation of the greater local initiation of innovation in Financial Services than in Data Processing is that the culture of the marketing group may encourage the continual development of "new products" to a greater extent than the one in Data Processing.

Three of the eight innovations had been initiated previously somewhere within VIC. It is no accident that Financial Services was the first unit to volunteer to adopt quality circles, as it had experimented with them through the now defunct "Participation Through Job Involvement" program. The unsuccessful piloting of staggered hours at headquarters may have paved the way for flextime. By the time flextime was adopted, a few key changes involving management control over workers, such as job posting and the open salary system, had also become accepted at headquarters. These changes may have made the organization more conducive to give workers greater control over their work day. The public giving of cash awards could be viewed as the next stage in the evolution of an open salary system. VIC had a secret bonus system in the past. Now that the open posting of job openings and salary levels had become commonplace, VIC was ready to initiate the award of public bonuses.

Table 3.12 summarizes some of the key implementation features of the innovations. Six of the eight innovations can be classified as having an active communication strategy; two programs, flexible benefits and cash awards, were classified as having a passive strategy. Passive strategies involved only written communication of the innovation like a memorandum or an article buried in the company newspaper. In contrast, active strategies included the use of training, discussions, meetings, presentations, and the public display of key symbols of the innovation like the opening of a fitness center.

As a review of the innovation's owner column suggests, local ownership is

Table 3.12
Key Adoption Features: Implementation

INNOVATION	COMMUNICATION STRATEGY	CURRENT USAGE PERCENT	OWNER(S)	CURRENT MANAGEMENT ATTENTION
JOB POSTING	active	10%* 3%*	local & headquarters	low
QUALITY CIRCLES	active	10%* 16%**	local	low
FLEXTIME	active	86%* 100%**	headquarters	low
NEWSLETTER	active	100%**	local	medium
PEER RECOGNITION	active	6%**	local	low
FITNESS PROGRAM	active	100%	local & headquarters	high
CASH AWARDS	passive	5% 2%**	local	medium
FLEXIBLE BENEFITS	passive	2%	headquarters	low

Key: * - Data Processing

  ** = Financial Services

  Percentages without * represent total for both departments.

imperative for the successful implementation of an active communication strategy. In some cases, sole local ownership may be preferred over joint corporate and local ownership, as some of the stories of adoption in this chapter suggest that the negative aspects of the politics of department and headquarters relations can sometimes get in the way of program implementation. Local and headquarters politics, for example, played a role in the slow implementation of cash awards in Financial Services.

The level of current top management attention to the innovation can be classified as low, medium, or high. Not surprisingly, the fitness center, the only
innovation studied that was clearly related to the organization's financial mission,
was the only human resource innovation that received high top management
attention.

The current annual percentage of employees using each innovation out of the
total eligible was computed by the researcher, and breakdowns by department
are given where appropriate. Some of the innovations that were administratively
imposed on all employees, such as flextime in Financial Services, the Taking
Care newsletter, or the *Grapevine*, have an official 100% participation rate.
However, these percentages do not necessarily represent 100% acceptance or
actual usage of the innovations. For example, every employee may receive a
Taking Care newsletter at home; however, every employee may not necessarily
read it.

A greater percentage of employees use job posting and have received cash
awards in Data Processing than in Financial Services. In contrast, a greater
percentage of employees are officially members of quality circles in Financial
Services than in Data Processing. However, as the results of the questionnaire
discussed in the next chapter suggest, the company records are out of date with
current use of some innovations.

Table 3.13 summarizes adoption features related to the diffusion or permeation
of the innovation and the level of official organizational support. The researcher
made determinations on whether six of the innovations had diffused to any other
parts of the organization. For cash awards and flexible benefits, it was not
appropriate to classify the diffusion of the innovation, since the adoption of these
programs was administratively imposed by the corporate level. Of the six innovations classified, only the employee-run newsletter had failed to diffuse to
any part of the firm.

An analysis was also made on whether the innovation had permeated or
significantly affected other parts of the human resource system. The newsletter,
the peer recognition program, flexible benefits, and cash awards have had little
impact on other areas of the human resource system and virtually exist as programs unto themselves. In contrast, the fitness center, quality circles, job posting,
and flextime have permeated the human resource system. The extent of permeation of these innovations has been classified as being a little, some, or a lot.

Quality circles have had only a little permeation, which may soon be rejected
by the personnel system. Originally, the corporate suggestion committee had
decided to allow quality circle suggestions to be eligible for financial remuneration under the company suggestion plan. As stated in the history of adoption
earlier in this chapter, however, it appears that circle suggestions are soon to be
deemed ineligible for the suggestion plan.

Job posting has had some permeation. This innovation has caused the salary
system to change from being closed to open for positions up to but not officer
and manager jobs. Only flextime and Taking Care have had a lot of permeation.

Table 3.13
Key Adoption Features: Level of Organizational Support

INNOVATION	DIFFUSION	PERMEATION	DOLLARS SPENT AS OF 9/86	NUMBER OF STAFF
JOB POSTING	yes	yes (some)	$20,000	8
QUALITY CIRCLES	yes	yes	$87,000	4
FLEXTIME	yes (a lot)	yes	$0	1
NEWSLETTER	no	no	$14,000	1
PEER RECOGNITION	yes	no	$6,000	1
FITNESS PROGRAM	yes (a lot)	yes	$6,500,000	4
CASH AWARDS	not applicable	no	$307,000	2
FLEXIBLE BENEFITS	not applicable	no	$450,000	2

Flextime has had a major impact on the first line supervisor's day-to-day man-agement of VIC employees. Flextime has changed the basic rules regarding the supervision of when an employee comes and leaves the workplace and when he or she goes to lunch. Taking Care also has had a lot of permeation. The evaluation of the innovation's level of success on influencing the behavior of VIC employees will be used as data to support the marketing of similar products to customer organizations. Even the fitness center will be used as a sterling example of one of the actions a customer should take to stop the rise in benefits costs.

The number of staff officially assigned to support the operation of the inno-vation and an estimate of the nonsalaried dollars spent on the innovation since its inception are also shown in Table 3.13. In terms of the official number of staff members, job posting has the highest head count, and flextime, the newsletter, and peer recognition have the lowest. It is interesting to note, however, that one reason the official head count may be small for many of the innovations is because committees are used to run them. As a consequence, participants' participation are not considered an official part of their jobs (e.g., the *Grapevine* editorial staff, the Taking Care working committees).

As for financial support, the organization clearly has spent the most money on Taking Care, which is the innovation with objectives that are closest to the financial goals of the firm and has received the most top management attention. It is useful to observe that one of the most successful innovations, flextime, cost no budgeted corporate money to implement.

NOTES

1. E. Rogers, *Diffusion of Innovations*, 3rd ed. (New York: Free Press, 1983), 363.

2. R. Walton, "The Diffusion of New Work Structures: Explaining Why Success Didn't Take," *Organizational Dynamics* 3 (1975): 22.

3. J. R. Kimberly, "Managerial Innovation," in P. Nystrom and W. Starbuck, eds., *Handbook of Organizational Design* (Oxford: Oxford University Press, 1981), 185.

4. E. E. Lawler, *High-Involvement Management* (San Francisco, Jossey-Bass, 1986), 64.

5. W. Pollack, and R. Stack, *Survey of National Corporations on Health Care Cost Containment* (Minneapolis: National Association of Employers on Health Care Alternatives, 1982).

6. P. J. DiMaggio, and W. W. Powell, "The Iron Cage Revisited: Institutional Isomorphism and Collective Rationality in Organizational Fields," *American Sociological Review* 48 (1983), 147–160.

4

Human Resource Innovation Survey Results

Gimmicks don't work! Most people want to do a good job—it is up to
management to help them, not discourage them by gimmicks. Try being
more communicative and honest in dealing with employees; skip the fancy
words and programs! You might be surprised by the results!

An anonymous Financial Services employee

The preceding remark was written by an employee on a questionnaire and gives
a flavor of the general response of VIC employees to many new personnel
practices. Similarly, the purpose of this chapter is to give a flavor of employee
reactions to the eight innovations through examination of frequencies and percentages of the responses to the questionnaire. This general discussion prepares
the way for the statistical analyses of employee differences in acceptance across
innovations that follows in chapter 5.

RESPONDENT BACKGROUND INFORMATION

The HRM innovation survey, found in the Appendix, was distributed to all
headquarters employees in the Financial Services and Data Processing departments. Out of 3551 questionnaires, 2094 were returned over several weeks,
giving a population response rate of 59%.

Table 4.1
Responses by Department

DEPARTMENT	NUMBER SENT	NUMBER RECEIVED	RESPONSE RATE
1. DATA PROCESSING	2526	1610	64%
2. FINANCIAL SERVICES	926	408	44%
MARKETING GROUP HUMAN RESOURCES	99	76	77%
TOTAL FINANCIAL SERVICES	1025	484	47%
QUESTIONNAIRE TOTAL	3551	2094	59%

Table 4.1 summarizes the response rates by department and shows that the rate for Data Processing (64%) was much higher than for Financial Services (47%). It is believed that the lower response rate can be partially explained by its distribution during the reorganization and also the fact that results from surveys held in the past had not always been fed back to all employees.

Frequencies and percentages are given for the respondents' backgrounds by race, sex, salary grade, and years with the company in Table 4.2. In general, the sample appears to be representative of the employee population. Of the respondents, 1924 represented three main hierarchical groups based on salary level category. These groups were used in analyses to examine the hypothesis regarding differential hierarchical acceptance of HRM innovation and included: (1) nonexempts (n = 265), the lowest group of employees who mainly have clerical jobs involving processing paper involving insurance administration, (2) professionals (n = 1509), the middle group of employees who may have computer programming, actuarial, sales, customer service, or first level supervisory jobs, and (3) officers and managers (n = 150), the highest group of employees who are considered the executives of the firm. The remaining 94 participants did not report their salary level group. Over half (57%) of the respondents had

Table 4.2
Respondents' Biographical Information

1. SEX	Data Processing Number	Percent	Financial Services Number	Percent	TOTAL Number	Percent
Men	914	57	141	29	1055	50
Women	647	40	312	65	959	46
Missing data	49	3	31	6	80	4
	1610		484		2094	
2. RACE						
White	1449	90	408	84	1857	89
Black	64	4	30	6	94	5
Asian	25	2	5	1.5	30	1
Hispanic	11	1	6	1.5	17	.5
Amer. Ind.	5	.5	4	1	9	.5
Missing data	56	3	31	6	87	4
3. SALARY GRADE						
Nonexempt	127	8	157	32	284	14
Prof.	1320	82	232	48	1552	74
Officer	97	6	63	13	160	8
Missing data	66	4	32	7	98	4
4. YEARS WITH COMPANY						
< 1	141	9	44	9	185	9
1-5	569	35	103	21	672	32
6-10	400	25	98	20	498	24
11-15	178	11	87	18	265	12.5
>/=16	280	17	133	27	413	19.5
Missing data	42	3	19	5	61	3

Table 4.3
Number and Percent of Respondents Who Use the Innovations

INNOVATION	Number of Respondents Who Use	Percent of Total Respondents Who Use*
FLEXTIME	1744	83%
FITNESS PROGRAM	1614	77%
NEWSLETTER	338	70%**
JOB POSTING	1285	61%
PEER RECOGNITION	150	31%**
QUALITY CIRCLES	411	20%
CASH AWARD	340	16%
FLEXIBLE BENEFITS	61	3%

* Total number of respondents is 2094.

** Percentage of 484 respondents, the total for Financial Services.

worked for the company six or more years. Of the respondents, 93% were white, and about half (53%) were male.

INNOVATION USE

Table 4.3 summarizes the number and percentage of respondents who use the innovations. These statistics probably give a better snapshot of current employee participation than the company records described at the end of the preceding chapter, since records varied in the extent to which they were complete and up-to-date. The rationale for examining the extent to which an innovation is used by employees is that it probably is the ultimate indicator of acceptance, particularly when usage is left up to employee discretion. If an innovation is open to all employees and a high percentage of the respondents report that they not only like it but they use it as well, the innovation probably has high acceptance.

The most widely used innovation is flextime; 83% of the total respondents said they could usually work the noncore hours of their choice. Of responding Financial Services employees, 83% read the employee newsletter; 73% usually read the fitness newsletter. Job posting is the next most widely used innovation; 61% of the respondents have either posted for a job or hired a job poster. Of Financial Services respondents, 31% have either received a People Are Tops award or have nominated someone for an award. For the other innovations, 20% of respondents are directly involved with quality circles as members, leaders, facilitators, or steering committee members; 16% have either received or nominated someone for a cash award; and only 3% have used the Flexible Spending Account.

Table 4.4 gives a breakdown of the usage data summarized in Table 4.3 by organizational unit. Respondents could check as many categories as appropriate for each innovation. Thus there are qualitative differences in the ways in which an employee can be considered a user of an innovation. Receiving a cash award is a very different experience of "usership" than nominating someone for an award. It's informative to not only have a global picture of the percentage of responding employees that can be considered "users" of the innovations, but also to have an understanding of the composition of the user population's background. An examination of similarities and differences in the percentage of users of each innovation in each unit gives insight into differences in the levels of acceptance between units.

For half of the six common innovations (cash awards, job posting, cafeteria benefits), the percentages of employees in Financial Services and Data Processing that used them in each user category were very similar. As for differences, about twice the percentage of Financial Services employees indicated they were circle members than in Data Processing (23% versus 12%). Of Financial Services respondents, 82% said they usually read the fitness newsletter versus 76% for Data Processing, and 90% of Financial Services respondents said they could usually work the noncore hours of their choice versus 81% for Data Processing. (Data Processing has several hundred employees in the data center who are exempt from flextime.)

For two of the innovations, respondents could state whether they desired opportunities for increased usage. Of the respondents in Data Processing, 13%, and 9% of Financial Services respondents were not currently members of a circle, but would like to join one. Of Data Processing and Financial Services respondents, 64% and 61%, respectively, would read a bulletin board with a list of the Outstanding Achievement Award winners on it, should management post one in the future.

Table 4.4
Analysis of Use of Innovations by Unit

INNOVATION	Data Processing		Financial Services		TOTAL	
	Number	Percent*	Number	Percent**	Number	Percent
1.CASH AWARD						
Received	93	6	17	4	110	5
Nominated someone	178	11	52	11	230	11
Ineligible (on						
incentive plan)	40	3	20	4	60	3
If TOAAP names						
were posted,						
would read list.	1020	64	251	52	1271	61
2.FLEXTIME						
Can usually work						
hours of choice	1310	81	434	90	1744	83
Have restrictions						
on choice of hours	149	9	35	7	184	9
Ineligible	93	6	.	.	93	6
3.QUALITY CIRCLES						
Circle member	200	12	95	23	295	14
Facilitator	19	1	10	3	29	1
Leader	35	2	23	6	58	3
Steering Committee/						
Administration	22	1	7	2	29	1
Read Newsletter	594	37	88	22	682	33
Not in circle, but						
would like to join	215	13	38	9	253	12
4.FITNESS PROGRAM						
Usually read						
newsletter	1215	76	399	82	1614	77
Signed up for						
fitness center	646	40	172	36	818	39
Watched video	224	14	95	20	319	15
Participated in						
group activity	224	14	107	22	331	16
5.JOB POSTING						
Posted for job	651	40	185	38	836	40
Hired job poster	346	22	103	21	449	21
6.FLEXIBLE BENEFITS						
Used	45	3	16	4	61	3
7.PEER RECOGNITION*						
Nominated someone	.	.	105	26	105	22
Received	.	.	45	11	45	9
8.NEWSLETTER*						
Usually read	.	.	338	83	338	70
On staff	.	.	6	2	6	1

* Percent of 1610, the total number of Data Processing respondents.
** Percent of 484, the total number of Financial Services respondents.

FLEXTIME

Turning to the level of acceptance of each innovation, flextime is the most accepted innovation by VIC employees. As an employee wrote, ''I think flextime is the best program VIC has for its employees," and 91% of all respondents agreed with the item, "Overall, flextime is a great program and should be continued." Similarly, 95% of all respondents agreed with the statement, "Flextime has helped employees better integrate work with their private lives," which is the main reason that Corporate Personnel gave employees for its introduction.

It appears that flextime not only has a favorable impact on morale, but on productivity. Nearly half of the respondents (49%) agreed with the item, "Flextime has helped improve my productivity," and 41% of all respondents agreed with the statement, "Flextime affects my performance on the job." This latter agreement percentage was the highest of all of the innovations. For each of the others, no more than 17% of the respondents said the program affected their performance. In descending order, the specific percentages of agreement with the statement, "(innovation name) affects my performance on the job," are as follows: fitness program (17%), quality circles (17%), peer recognition award (13%), cash awards (12%), job posting (11%), newsletter (6%), and flexible benefits (1%).

Only two negative areas surfaced regarding flextime, which relate to either the placement of restrictions on certain employees' use of the innovations or to the longer lunch hour. Comments from questionnaires and group interviews suggest that it would be desirable to make flextime equally available to all employees. Excluding one or two groups for "business necessity" reasons, as Data Processing did for the data center, or placing limitations on some use of flextime, as Financial Services did for clerical employees, can have negative consequences for morale. Thirty-seven percent of respondents agreed with the statement, "It's not fair that some employees like (receptionists or data center workers) can't flex because they have to cover their work area." (In Data Processing, the words "data center workers" were inserted, whereas "receptionists" was inserted for Financial Services.) As one employee in the data center wrote, "In general, most of the "hype" and fanfare for all new programs are carried out in the main work areas. Few programs are ever put on in the data center."

As for the lunch hour, some employees would like to be given the choice of being able to take a 30-minute lunch, as they dislike the mandatory hour lunch period. For example, only 45% of the respondents agreed with the item, "It's good we have an hour lunch period, because almost everyone needs an hour for lunch."

JOB POSTING

Most of the respondents liked the idea of having openings within the company publicized via job posting. Nearly all of them (88%) agreed with the statement, "It's nice to know job posting is there." Seventy-five percent of respondents agreed with the item, "Job posting has given employees the opportunity to improve their own work situation," and 76% agreed with the item, "Overall, job posting is a great program and should be continued." It appears that, in general, employees believe their lives are better off with job posting than without it.

However, VIC management needs to work to improve the credibility of the system by making sure that employees believe that posted jobs are truly open to all interested applicants. Nearly half (44%) of respondents agreed with the item, "Often jobs are posted that are already filled." As a Financial Services employee wrote, "(We need to have) open job posting. Too many times an employee is chosen before a job is posted. Posting is done as a matter of formality." Similarly, a Data Processing employee wrote, "Job posting is generally a very good program except there is too much inter-area recruiting going on under the guise of posting, which is not fair to others who may be interested."

The results also portend the diffusion of job posting to officer and managerial positions. Despite the fact that officer jobs aren't currently posted, nearly half of the respondents (42%) agreed with the statement, "It would be good if officer jobs were posted." Although job posting is currently unavailable to their salary group, officers are more favorable about the innovation than any other group, as the results for the analysis of variance by salary group presented in the next chapter show.

The questionnaire results also suggest a need to make a change in the way the innovation is administered from using bulletin boards and a paper posting system toward a computerized one. This need is particularly salient in work areas within VIC where computers are prevalent such as Data Processing. Over three-fourths of Data Processing respondents (76%), for example, agreed with the empathic item, "It would be good if job announcements were available via a CRT." In addition, a decrease in the use of paper to administer job posting is a change that some VIC employees would welcome. A third of all respondents agreed with the statement, "The job posting procedure is too bureaucratic."

FITNESS PROGRAM

Nearly half of the respondents (49%) agreed with the statement, "The fitness center is the best feature of Taking Care." Whereas the actual acceptance of the multimillion-dollar fitness center cannot be fully assessed until it opens, the less costly tactic of mailing a newsletter home each month has been very effective; 77% of respondents reported that they usually read the fitness newsletter sent to their home. Similarly, 70% agreed with the statement, "I like to receive the Taking Care newsletter."

Employees are uncertain about the actual impact of the fitness program on their behavior. Whereas 58% of responding employees agreed with the item, "Taking Care has reinforced positive lifestyle and medical self-care," a goal of the program, a lower percentage (40%) agreed with the item, "Taking Care has improved the fitness of employees." An even smaller portion of respondents (29%) agreed with the statement, "Taking Care has saved VIC money by lowering health care costs," the innovation's primary objective.

The major complaints regarding Taking Care pertain to either the exclusion of employee groups from using the center or the requirement that employees must pay for their own physical in order to use the center. Regarding the latter, 39% of employees disagreed with the item, "People who want to use the fitness center should pay for their own physical."

Last, new and part-time employees are unhappy about their exclusion from using the center. As the analysis of variance results by years of service presented in the next chapter show, new employees have the least favorable attitudes toward Taking Care. Comments made in group interviews and on questionnaires suggest that these attitudes are because new employees are excluded from using the center.

The exclusion of part-time employees from the on-site fitness center is a visible reminder of their second-class status at VIC. As one part-time employee wrote, "Part time employees in Data Processing have full professional responsibilities, but are not eligible for many of these programs. The official explanation for ineligibility is always 'the company wants to provide incentives for employees to work full-time,' but the decision to work part-time is usually based on private considerations, not availability of incentive programs."

QUALITY CIRCLES

A recent review of the effectiveness of employee involvement programs concluded that as long as quality circles are viewed as programs, they are likely to ultimately fail, and VIC's experiences with them appear to reflect this observation.[1] Attitudes toward the innovation were relatively lukewarm. Only a third of the respondents (34%) felt that Innovation Through Involvement has helped make employees more involved in their jobs. Only 17% of responding employees agreed with the statement, "Innovation Through Involvement is very important to me." A third of the respondents agreed with the item, "It wouldn't bother me if Innovation Through Involvement were discontinued."

In the next chapter, the results of the analysis of variance between employees who use the innovation and those who do not, and analysis of significant differences between users in each department are discussed in detail. The results show that users of quality circles have significantly greater acceptance than nonusers and that Data Processing users are significantly more favorable than Financial Services users. Even within the Data Processing user group, however, it appears that circle members are less enthusiastic than the facilitators or managers of the innovation. In Data Processing all of the responding quality circle facilitators agreed with the item, "In general, Innovation Through Involvement is a great program and should be continued," whereas only 82% of circle members did so. Similarly, none of the facilitators agreed with the statement, "It wouldn't bother me if Innovation Through Involvement were discontinued," whereas one-fifth (19%) of circle members did.

Only 12% of the respondents agreed with the statement, "Participation in

Innovation Through Involvement is voluntary,'' which refers to a key precept of the program. There appears to be some problems in implementing the goal of voluntary participation. For example, one Financial Services employee commented, "When I was in the Administration and Customer Services division, I was told that I had to be a leader because I was a supervisor. The program is supposed to be voluntary. Since I've joined Marketing, I have not been invited to join a group, although the people in my unit belong to an Innovation Through Involvement group. So in Administration and Customer Services, I was forced to join a group and in Marketing, I can't join a group. *Some voluntary program.*"

Employees have also commented on other problems related to the poor administration of quality circles, which illustrate the way in which an innovation can lower employee acceptance of not only the innovation, but also of the whole human resource system of the organization. As one employee wrote:

I also know for a fact that at least *two* presentations that were accepted by management have never really been put into production. These two Innovation Through Involvement groups are still active, but if you check the membership, you will find that none of the original members are still there. There was an article about one of the groups in the Innovation Through Involvement newsletter stating how great their suggestion was and how the group is still together. This was a very misleading article due to the fact that all of the original members involved in the presentation were no longer in the group. The only thing that remained the same was the name. I believe that the concept is great, but our program at VIC needs a great deal of improvement. The competitions that were run in 1985 between group presentations defeated the whole idea of quality circles. I was a part of one of those groups and was told that all participants would receive a gift. I never did receive that gift.

CASH AWARDS

VIC's adoption of cash awards is indicative of the current organizational trend to make an increasing percentage of an organization's compensation system variable as opposed to fixed.[2] The results on the acceptance of cash awards at VIC must be viewed in light of the facts that VIC's program is less than a year old and is not well publicized in pockets of the organization. Nevertheless, it is clear that most employees would like cash awards to be better publicized. A large majority of respondents (74%) agreed with the statement, "I'd like to know more about who won the award and what they did." Similarly, 51% of the respondents disagreed with the statement, "In general, communication on the Outstanding Achievement Award program has been good." As one employee wrote, "Too little has been said about the Outstanding Achievement Awards. Recipients should be recognized publicly, i.e., in the company newspaper."

Despite employee interest in having the innovation better publicized, the respondents do not have highly favorable attitudes toward cash awards. Only 22% of the respondents agreed with the statement, "The Outstanding Achievement Award program is very important to me." Only slightly more than a fourth of the respondents (27%) agreed with the item, "It would bother me if the Outstanding Achievement Award program were discontinued." However, over a third of the respondents (38%) agreed with the statement, "A lot of improvement should be made in the way the Outstanding Achievement Award program is run." The program may have had a negative impact on the morale of some workers, as 38% of the respondents disagreed with the statement, "This program has made me more motivated in my work."

Many employees would like to see the innovation redesigned to focus more on group achievements than individual ones; 62% of respondents agreed with the item, "The Outstanding Achievement Award program should recognize group achievements as well as individual ones." Forty percent of the respondents disagreed with the statement, "The Outstanding Achievement Award program helps create a team atmosphere," which refers to one of the formal corporate goals of the innovation.

A large minority of employees believe that the cash awards are not fairly distributed. Over a third (38%) of the respondents agreed with the statement, "People who work in lower level jobs are less likely to get an Outstanding Achievement Award," and 43% agreed with the statement, "Getting a cash award largely depends on your boss's sales ability." Only 24% of the respondents agreed with the sentence, "Deserving employees have received this award." As an employee wrote, "Regarding cash awards, it seems awards are given for *just showing up at work.* It's a good program in concept, but is *not* well respected because of poor administration."

Another employee wrote, "People get the award who don't deserve it, i.e., for doing their "assigned" job they got an award. Special projects, although it is an assigned task, usually gets an award. People working hard in operations and maintenance areas don't get anything but grief! Better and stricter rules are needed for who gets an award. Maybe management by peers rather than "snowed" senior management would be best."

FLEXIBLE BENEFITS

VIC's experience with flexible benefits highlights the importance of conducting a lot of internal employee market research before designing such an innovation. Clearly, the design of the innovation, not necessarily the idea of flexible benefits, is what employees do not like about the Flexible Spending Account. For example, over half of the respondents (55%) agreed with the statement, "The use it or lose it rule discourages me from signing up for the Flexible Spending Account," which refers to a key feature of the innovation. Similarly, over two-thirds (67%) of the respondents agreed with the item, "It's too difficult to predict your health care expenses not covered by the regular policy a year in advance." Sixty-four percent of the respondents agreed with the statement, "The Flexible Spending Account has little importance to me."

It appears that many of the respondents dislike not only key features of the program, but also the entire design of VIC's employee benefits package. Over a quarter of the respondents (28%) disagreed with the statement, "VIC's benefits package fits my needs." An employee wrote this comment, which is typical of a number that were made: "The insurance benefits at VIC are the poorest of any company I have known. For an insurance company, we should be ashamed." A significant minority of respondents are cynical about the company's motives for introducing the Flexible Spending Account, as over a quarter (26%) agreed with the statement, "This program is designed to make VIC money."

The lack of acceptance of the Flexible Spending Account by some employees probably can be attributed to a lack of employee familiarity with the innovation and the ineffectiveness of Corporate Personnel's communication efforts. Over a quarter of the respondents (29%) disagreed with the statement, "I am familiar with the main features of the Flexible Spending Account." In addition, 40% of the respondents disagreed with the statement, "In general, communication on the Flexible Spending Account has been good." One employee left the page on the Flexible Spending Account blank and scrawled this comment on the bottom: "I don't understand this program at all! This should have been introduced to groups of employees at seminars."

PEER RECOGNITION AWARD

Financial Services employees are reasonably accepting of the People Are Tops program, as 58% of the respondents agreed with the statement, "In general, People Are Tops is a great program and should be continued." A majority of respondents believe the award is appropriately administered. Sixty percent of the respondents agreed with the statement, "Deserving employees have received this award." Financial Services employees are very familiar with this innovation; 76% agreed with the statement, "I am familiar with the main features of the People Are Tops program."

Despite the favorable attitudes that are held by a majority of employees, a substantial minority have negative impressions of the innovation. A little less than a third of respondents agreed with the statement, "It wouldn't bother me if People Are Tops were discontinued." Over a third of the respondents agreed with the statement, "The fun and games that can go with announcing the People Are Tops award sometimes take away from its sincerity." Over a fifth of employees disagreed with the statement, "The People Are Tops program motivates employees to apply their best effort," which refers to one of the formal goals of the innovation. A fifth of the respondents (20%) agreed with the statement, "A lot of improvement should be made in the way People Are Tops is run."

Some employees feel the award is a management attempt to avoid paying money to outstanding performers. As one employee wrote: "Rather than give People Are Tops awards, why not give these people raises, which they more than deserve for their *continuous* contributions." Another employee wrote:

Management's efforts in motivating employees and rewarding performance seems misguided. *Incentive programs* designed to give due "recognition" for good service *are merely* bureaucratic *smoke screens for a poor wage structure* system. If employees felt fairly compensated for their efforts, turnover would decrease; generally the less talented employees remain loyal to VIC because they have few alternatives in the marketplace. People Are Tops awards are pure *tinsel* and do not adequately address the non-competitive salary system.

As these results and those from the case history of the recognition award suggest, it appears that Financial Services managers will have difficulty in successfully maintaining a high profile for the awards and sustaining organizational enthusiasm. Whereas top management recognition and support of the need to "reintroduce People Are Tops" may be helpful in the short term, it appears that competition from another innovation, the cash awards, is likely to pose future problems for the health of the program.

EMPLOYEE NEWSLETTER

The employee newsletter seems to be very successful, as 83% of Financial Services respondents said they usually read the *Grapevine*. (This percentage is remarkably high considering the fact that the innovation was discontinued for six months due to the reorganization, and only one issue had come out since its reinitiation and the administration of the questionnaire.) Of responding employees, 51% agreed with the statement, "Overall, I like the way the *Grapevine* is designed," and 55% agreed with the statement, "I find the *Grapevine* very entertaining." A sizable minority (43%) agreed with the item, "The *Grapevine* is a lot more interesting to read than other company publications."

Results were mixed on the extent to which respondents believe that the *Grapevine* has achieved its objectives. Whereas 54% of the respondents agreed with the statement, "The *Grapevine* helps recognize peoples' achievements," 45% disagreed with the statement, "It helps me feel closer to the senior vice president and his staff."

Last, there are important differences between employees with varying years of service in their acceptance of the *Grapevine*. As the results of the analysis of variance by years of service show in the next chapter, the innovation is a good orientation device for newer employees. Employees with one to five years of service were the most favorable of all of the years of service groups.

WORK ENVIRONMENT

Because it was believed that employees' acceptance of the innovations would be influenced by their general attitudes toward VIC's working environment, a section with statements pertaining to the organizational climate was included at the end of the survey, which can be found in the Appendix. Some of these statements were developed as a result of employee interviews and some were taken from previous opinion surveys conducted at VIC. Highlights of employees' responses to this section are given below.

A majority of the respondents have favorable attitudes regarding the way their supervisors threat them; 64% of respondents agreed with the statement, "My supervisor recognizes and appreciates good work and tells us so." Fifty-five percent agreed with the statement, "My immediate supervisor places a high priority on my personal work needs," and 65% of responding employees disagreed with the item, "I often doubt the truth of what my supervisor tells me." Fifty-three percent of the respondents agreed with the statement, "In general, my supervisor is open to progressive people practices," and 76% agreed with the statement, "I respect my immediate supervisor."

Employees hold less favorable opinions regarding top management; 43% of the respondents agreed and 22% disagreed with the statement, "(Data Processing or Financial Services) top management is interested in the welfare and overall satisfaction of those who work here." Of responding employees, 34% agreed and 20% disagreed with the statement, "The head of (Financial Services or Data Processing) is very concerned about the needs of employees." Thirty-eight percent of respondents agreed and 70% disagreed with the item, "(The VIC chairman's name) really cares about employee welfare."

A majority of employees do not hold favorable opinions regarding the Personnel department and its programs. Only 38% of responding employees agreed with the statement, "(Financial Services or Data Processing) Human Resources does a good job of carrying out programs." Only 29% of respondents agreed with the statement, "The Corporate Personnel department does a good job of administering programs." Nearly a third of the respondents (31%) agreed with the statement, "A lot of personnel programs come and go around here." Only 21% of the respondents agreed with the statement, "Most of the personnel programs that are tried in my division are successful," and 38% disagreed with the item, "From what I know, personnel policies are uniformly administered from division to division."

Last, it appears that the empathic questionnaire was taken seriously by employees; 72% of respondents agreed with the statement, "Filling out this survey is a good way to let management know how I feel about these programs." However, respondents were considerably less optimistic about the likelihood that management would take action in response to the results. Only 34% of the respondents agreed with the statement, "(Data Processing or Financial Services) management will carefully consider problems brought to its attention by this survey."

NOTES

1. E. E. Lawler, *High-Involvement Management* (San Francisco: Jossey-Bass, 1986), 64.

2. R. M. Kanter, "The Attack on Pay," *Harvard Business Review* (March 1967), 60–67.

5

Toward a Theory of Acceptance of Human Resource Innovation: The Effects of Hierarchical Level, Organizational Unit, and Innovation Type

MEASURING EFFECTIVENESS OF INNOVATION

A. Tsui and G. Milkovich[1] have developed a multiple constituency approach for evaluating Human Resource Management (HRM) effectiveness, which is defined as the extent to which personnel activities meet constituency expectations. The current study suggests that some past studies evaluating innovative HRM programs (e.g., quality circles, drug testing) conducted with one or two senior managers per firm (e.g., selected from a roster of American Society of Personnel Administrators or a listing of the Fortune 500) may have overstated their effectiveness.[2] Whereas such research provides valuable insight into senior managers' perceptions of effectiveness and presents the views of a key constituency, little understanding of the level of program acceptance and use by the main constituents (employees) is offered. Assessments of the programs may be influenced by the different organizational positions that company executives and employees hold. Executives make or influence HR policy decisions; their subordinates simply use the programs. Because of these differences, executives may wish to project their firm's HR program favorably in order to promulgate the company's reputation.

The current study examines this variation in perceptions of HR program effectiveness across organizational levels and other background characteristics, as well as between organizational units and various HRM innovations. Effectiveness of the innovation is measured in terms of the extent of acceptance. Some scholars have suggested that acceptance is as good a measure of effectiveness as more "objective" ones, such as return on investment and other productivity statistics,[3] which have the possibility of being even harder to disentangle than member assessments.[4] Also, research investigating motivational influences on training program effectiveness has found, for example, that positive employee reactions to a program precede behavior change and improvements in job-related outcomes.[5] A richer understanding of the factors associated with varying levels of HRM acceptance is needed, since HRM programs are rarely completely accepted or rejected.

OBJECTIVES AND HYPOTHESES

The objectives of this chapter are to systematically examine the relationship between employee hierarchical level and other background characteristics (race, sex, seniority, program experience, organizational unit) and acceptance of eight innovative HRM programs. The purpose is to extend our understanding of HRM innovation by providing insight into whether senior level employees tend to perceive HR innovations to be more effective than employees at lower levels, as well as to examine the influence of other background characteristics on HRM attitudes.

Unlike most past work on innovation, this research investigates the *effects* of organizational innovations on its members. Whether an employee is male or female, black or white, manager or clerk will have important influences on his or her work experiences, which will affect his or her attitudes toward the human resource system. Surely these differences in employee backgrounds will also influence attitudes toward new work programs that are adopted.

By studying eight innovations representing a sampling of programs in an organization's human resources system, an attempt is also made to understand how acceptance of innovation might vary for different kinds of personnel innovations. Previous work has tended to make distinctions only between organizational and technological innovations. Yet there is wide diversity in the nature of innovations included within each of these categories. Thus the analyses in this chapter also explore the issue of whether acceptance of innovation might be affected by the social properties of the innovations themselves.

Influence of Hierarchical Level

Research conducted over several decades consistently indicates a positive association between hierarchical level and favorable workplace attitudes.[6] The need to investigate the relationship between level and attitudes toward HRM programs is highlighted by Tsui's and Milkovich's preliminary finding that the largest difference in constituent preferences for Personnel department activities was between executives and hourly employees.[7] In addition, studies of hierarchical differences in perceptions of specific HRM programs, such as performance appraisals, for example, have found that managers are consistently more favorable than subordinates, perhaps due in part to the different roles each group has in using appraisals.[8] Last, research has shown that organizational level is a better predictor of positive work attitudes than other background variables such as gender or marital status.[9] In concert with this prior research, the main hypothesis examined in this chapter is that hierarchical level is positively related to acceptance of HRM innovation.

Effects of Race and Sex

It is also useful to assess whether membership in employee groups protected by federal equal employment opportunity legislation (e.g., race, sex) is related to attitudes toward HRM programs. It is proposed that female and minority employees will be less accepting of HRM innovations adopted by senior management, which is typically white male. Women and minorities tend to hold predominately lower level and less desirable positions in corporate America, which may negatively influence their work attitudes.[10] These employees might also face greater risks in actively embracing innovative HRM programs than their white male counterparts who may be more secure partially because they do not have the added pressures of possibly encountering racism and sexism in the workplace.

Seniority

Employee seniority, another important background variable, is hypothesized to be negatively related to acceptance. The longer that employees work for a company, the less accepting they might be of changes in the HRM system and the less of a stake they might have in supporting changes affecting the organization's future. A recent study on attitudes toward quality circles found that senior employees had less favorable attitudes than junior ones for some of these very reasons.[11]

Influence of Program Experience

The variable of program experience allows for incorporation of behavioral measures into the analyses. It is expected that program experience will be positively related to acceptance. Although companies offer a multitude of personnel programs to a variety of constituencies, not all employees are equally involved with them. Some HRM programs exclude certain employee groups (e.g., executives) by design such as quality circles. Others are optional in use, such as fitness programs or flexible benefits. The study of program experience also allows for exploration into whether there are any types of HRM programs, which exclude high level employees by design (e.g., quality circles, recognition programs), that might receive greater acceptance by excluded groups than employees in targeted groups (e.g., low level employees). Employees who have had direct contact with the innovations are believed to possess more accepting attitudes than those who have never used them, which either assumes that using programs is positively reinforcing or that employees with accepting attitudes are more predisposed to use the programs in the first place. Although exploration of the relationship between program experience and attitudes allowed for integration of behavioral measures into the research, the intent is merely to indicate the existence of a relationship, *not* to signify causal direction.

Organizational Unit

The last variable, organizational unit, is studied in order to assess variation in acceptance between the Data Processing and Financial Services departments. As the case histories of the adoption of each innovation in chapter 3 show, human resource innovations can be administered in very different ways in different organizational units. Consequently, it is believed that organizational unit membership might be an important influence on the level of acceptance between departments. Because of these interunit differences in implementation, however, organizational unit was controlled for within subjects analyses involving the effects of innovation, hierarchical level, race, sex, seniority, and program experience.

CHARACTERISTICS OF MEASURES

The percentages and frequencies summarizing employee responses to the empathic questionnaire items in the preceding chapter provide rich insight into the differing employee responses to the innovations. However, one of the main objectives of this research was also to understand differences in the level of acceptance across innovations. Consequently, it is necessary to use common items for the analysis. This section includes descriptions of the attitude toward HRM innovation scale, and also other variables that were used in the analyses to measure employee backgrounds and attitudes toward the work environment.

Attitude Toward HRM Innovation

Table 5.1 shows means and standard deviations for the ten common items comprising the attitude toward HRM innovation scale, introduced in chapter 2. Employee responses to the items, which used a five-point Likert-type scale (1 = strongly agree; 5 = strongly disagree), were summed (reversing negatively worded ones) to measure acceptance of each program.

In order to make comparisons across innovations, it is necessary to not only use common items, but also reliable ones. Reliability analysis was conducted separately on each scale, using Cronbach's Coefficient Alpha, an estimate of

Table 5.1

Item Means and Standard Deviations for the Attitude Toward HRM Innovation Scale by Program (5-point scale: 1 = Strongly Agree, 5 = Strongly Disagree)

	Flextime		Job Posting		Fitness Program		Quality Circles		Flexible Benefits		Cash Award		News Letter		Peer Award	
	M	SD	M	SD	M	SD	M	SD	M	SD	M	SD	M	SD	M	SD
1. I am familiar with the main features of (Innovation Name).	1.48	.63	2.28	.80	2.20	.82	2.43	1.02	2.78	1.12	2.95	1.17	2.36	.81	2.14	.76
2. (Innov. Name) is very important to me.	1.73	.96	2.61	.88	2.72	.96	3.22	.97	3.76	.89	3.00	.86	3.05	.96	3.12	.95
3. (Innov. Name) of little importance to me.*	4.10	1.05	3.54	.89	3.35	.98	2.91	1.05	2.15	.98	2.94	.96	3.10	.96	3.16	.96
4. Overall, I think (Innov. Name) is very well run.	2.09	.83	2.88	.80	3.32	.69	2.88	.79	3.11	.56	3.17	.76	2.48	.73	2.66	.78
5. A lot of improvement should be made in the way (Innov. Name) is run.*	3.51	.87	2.63	.88	3.03	.70	2.85	.81	2.74	.66	2.53	.83	3.20	.75	3.00	.80
6. I like (Innov. Name)'s design.	1.95	.76	2.61	.82	2.58	.70	2.77	.79	3.23	.72	3.02	.76	2.39	.72	2.62	.79
7. My supervisor supports (Innov. Name).	1.82	.74	2.38	.74	2.68	.67	2.53	.83	2.95	.53	2.52	.78	2.68	.64	2.30	.80
8. In general, communication on (Innov. Name) has been good.	2.05	.76	2.89	.88	2.28	.78	2.90	.91	3.27	.99	3.60	.95	2.42	.74	2.47	.87
9. Overall, (Innov. Name) is a great program & should be continued.	1.51	.73	2.03	.76	2.35	.85	2.52	.89	3.11	.73	2.73	.83	2.48	.81	2.34	.89
10. It wouldn't bother me if (Innov. Name) were discontinued.*	4.23	1.10	3.91	.97	3.42	1.08	2.92	1.07	2.28	.94	3.03	1.04	3.20	1.05	3.14	1.07

Table 5.2
Characteristics of Measures

(Using a 5 point scale: 1 = strongly agree to 5 = strongly disagree; means ranked from the most favorable to the most unfavorable)

INNOVATION	MEAN	SD	ALPHA COEF.	MEAN INTER-ITEM CORRELATION
FLEXTIME	1.88	.58	.87	.41
JOB POSTING	2.56	.51	.81	.30
FITNESS PROGRAM	2.57	.58	.88	.43
PEER RECOGNITION	2.64	.60	.87	.41
NEWSLETTER	2.63	.60	.91	.50
QUALITY CIRCLES	2.86	.64	.88	.43
CASH AWARDS	3.05	.57	.83	.35
FLEXIBLE BENEFITS	3.30	.44	.72	.24

WORK ENVIRONMENT

KEY SUBCOMPONENTS				
IMMEDIATE SUPERVISOR (10 items)	2.45	.72	.91	.50
TOP MANAGEMENT (2 items)	2.56	.75	.69	.53
PERSONNEL DEPARTMENT (3 items)	2.74	.62	.75	.50
GLOBAL WORK ENVIRONMENT (38 items)	2.68	.53	.95	.32

reliability based on item intercorrelations.[12] Table 5.2 shows the means, standard deviations, alpha coefficients, and the mean intercorrelations for the items used in the scales.

The scale was found to be very reliable across innovations, as the reliabilities ranged from .91 to .72. The comparable scales were not strongly correlated (mean r = .19). Due to the exploratory nature of the study and its main objectives, which were to examine variation in acceptance of innovation across employee groups and personnel programs and analyses indicating that the items held together best as an overall attitude toward HRM innovation scale, a decision was made to collapse the scales to represent a general attitude toward personnel innovation.

Employee Background Variables

Questionnaire data on respondent use of the programs and their backgrounds were categorized in the following manner for the statistical analyses in this chapter: hierarchical level (salary grade group = nonexempt, professionals, officers, and managers); race (caucasian/noncaucasian); sex; years with the company (≤ 1, 1–5, 6–10, 11–15, ≥ 16), program experience (user/nonuser), and organizational unit (Financial Services, Data Processing). It is important to note that although efforts were made to conduct analyses by specific minority subgroups (e.g., black, Asian, Hispanic), it was necessary to form a dichotomous race variable because of the very small number of individuals in each subgroup. Similarly, program experience was analyzed using a dichotomous variable because of the theoretical difficulties in comparing multiple and different types of uses across multiple innovations.

Attitudes Toward the Overall Work Environment

All of these innovations are administered as part of VIC's system of human resource management. Employee attitudes toward these programs are undoubtedly going to be influenced by their perceptions of the overall working environment and attitudes toward key players who administer or represent the organization's philosophy of human resources management. To what extent do VIC employees hold favorable attitudes toward their work environment or such key players as top management, supervisors, and the personnel department?

To answer the first part of this question, 38 items with factor loadings of greater than .3 from the work environment/climate section were summed to create an overall mean representing the level of favorable attitudes toward the work environment. Like the means developed for acceptance of innovation, the closer that the mean is to 1, the greater the acceptance. As the mean of 2.68 in Table 5.2 suggests, employees do not hold overwhelmingly favorable attitudes toward the overall work environment.

Analysis was also done on three subcomponents of the work environment section that were believed could be distinguished by their content. These include statements about employees' relationships with their supervisors, their perceptions of top management, and their attitudes toward the personnel department. Employees hold the most favorable attitudes toward their supervisors, top management ranks next, and the Personnel department is last. Although the study was not formally conducted to determine the extent to which the Personnel department's stature is related to the acceptance of innovation, it was based on the implicit assumption that an organization's tendency to have high acceptance of innovation is dependent on whether it has a Personnel department that is viewed favorably.

To what extent are employees' attitudes toward the work environment related to their attitudes toward personnel innovations? Table 5.3 shows the correlations between the measures of acceptance of innovation and the measures of the work environment. There is a moderate positive relationship between employees' attitudes toward the work environment and their attitudes toward the innovations. It is also interesting to observe that attitudes toward one of the innovations, the People Are Tops award, appeared to be a good predictor of attitudes toward most of the other innovations. A positive attitude toward People Are Tops was moderately positively correlated with the other programs.

INNOVATION DIFFERENCES

Overview of Statistical Analyses

Using a within-subjects design and controlling for organizational unit, analyses of variance were conducted by salary level, race, sex, seniority, and program experience for the six innovations adopted in both Financial Services and Data Processing, which are shown in Table 5.4. The results are based on data for only the six common innovations as it was desirable to use as large a database as possible to explore theorized relationships.

Thus the database was arranged in two different ways for the statistical analyses. First, analysis was done using the large data set that combined the results on the acceptance of the six innovations adopted in both Data Processing and Financial Services. Then analysis was conducted on all eight innovations in the study using only Financial Services data, which can be found in Table 5.5. (In order to see whether the same significant results were found using data on the acceptance of all eight innovations, statistical analyses were also done using only data from Financial Services. As the results in Table 5.5 show, virtually all the same effects as those in the large data set were found in the smaller one with one exception. The innovation by race interaction was not significant, which may simply be a function of the smaller number of minority employees in the data set.)

The Influence of Innovation Type

Does acceptance of innovation differ between the programs? As the very large F value (876.87, $p < .0001$) for the within-subjects main effect of innovation indicates, the answer is resoundingly affirmative. Clearly, employees responded

Table 5.3
Correlations between Measures

VARIABLES	1.	2.	3.	4.	5.	6.	7.	8.	9.	10.	11.	12.
1. FLEXTIME	-											
2. JOB POSTING	.30[1]	-										
3. CASH AWARD	.05[3]	.18[1]	-									
4. FITNESS PROGRAM	.13[1]	.21[1]	.19[1]	-								
5. FLEXIBLE BENEFITS	.03	.09[2]	.17[1]	.19[1]	-							
6. QUALITY CIRCLES	.12[1]	.22[1]	.30[1]	.24[1]	.15[1]	-						
7. PEER AWARD	.21[1]	.44[1]	.42[1]	.25[1]	.13[3]	.30[1]	-					
8. NEWSLETTER	.09	.18[2]	.12[3]	.16[2]	.13[3]	.20[1]	.24[1]	-				
9. GLOBAL WORK ENVIRONMENT	.25[1]	.38[1]	.37[1]	.27[1]	.16[1]	.30[1]	.49[1]	.23[1]	-			
10. TOP MANAGEMENT	.18[1]	.27[1]	.33[1]	.24[1]	.14[1]	.28[1]	.36[1]	.20[1]	.68[1]	-		
11. SUPERVISOR	.21[1]	.27[1]	.24[1]	.14[1]	.09[2]	.19[1]	.33	.15[2]	.84[1]	.47[1]	-	
12. PERSONNEL DEPARTMENT	.16[1]	.27[1]	.21[1]	.28[1]	.18[1]	.23[1]	.20[1]	.25[1]	.54[1]	.54[1]	.38[1]	-

1= Significant at the P < .0001 level
2= Significant at the P < .001 level
3= Significant at the P < .05 level

very differently to each of the innovations, as the means in Table 5.2 indicate. It appears that the nature of the innovations themselves has the greatest influence on the extent to which they are accepted.

Acceptance significantly differed between nearly all the innovations in the study. With the lowest mean, flextime is by far the most preferred innovation. Job posting was next, followed by the fitness program, and then quality circles. Marketing employees rated the peer award and newsletter next. The least accepted

Table 5.4
Results of ANOVAS for Effects of Innovation and Employee Backgrounds on Acceptance of Six Innovations Controlling for Organizational Unit

SOURCE	DEGREES OF FREEDOM	F VALUE	PROB.> F
WITHIN SUBJECTS			
INNOVATION	(5, 8420)	876.87	O.O
INNOVATION. X UNIT	(5, 8450)	8.09	.0001
INNOVATION X GENDER	(5, 8185)	2.45	.03
INNOVATION X RACE	(5, 8160)	5.21	.0001
INNOVATION X SALARY	(10, 8125)	16.04	.0001
INNOVATION X YEARS	(20, 8240)	4.14	.0001
INNOVATION X GENDER X UNIT	(5, 8185)	.55	.74
INNOVATION X RACE X UNIT	(5, 8160)	.38	.86
INNOVATION X SALARY X UNIT	(10, 8185)	1.63	.09
INNOVATION X YEARS X UNIT	(20, 8240)	1.82	.01
PROGRAM EXPERIENCE	(1, 11874)	605.84	.0001
PROG. EXP. X INNOVATION	(5, 11874)	208.92	.0001
PROG. EXP X UNIT	(1, 11874)	7.24	.0071
PROG. EXP. X UNIT X INNOVATION	(5, 11874)	8.19	.0001
BETWEEN SUBJECTS			
UNIT	(1, 1690)	.74	.39
GENDER	(1, 1637)	.02	.88
RACE	(1, 1632)	1.78	.18
YEARS WITH COMPANY	(4, 1648)	.54	.71
SALARY GRADE	(2, 1625)	12.18	.0001
GENDER X UNIT	(1, 1637)	2.84	.09
RACE X UNIT	(1, 1632)	.15	.70
SALARY X UNIT	(2, 1625)	1.81	.16
YEARS X UNIT	(4, 1648)	.38	.82

innovations, which had the highest means indicating the least agreement with the statements, are the cash award and the flexible benefits programs. It is important to note that the innovation with the greatest acceptance is the one that can least be viewed as a "program," but rather as an operating procedure

Table 5.5
Results of ANOVAS for Effects of Innovation and Employee Backgrounds on
Acceptance of Eight Innovations Using Financial Services Data Only

SOURCE	DEGREES OF FREEDOM	F VALUE	PROB.> F
WITHIN SUBJECTS			
INNOVATION	(7, 1939)	150.60	O.O
INNOVATION X GENDER	(7, 1939)	2.42	.022
INNOVATION X RACE	(7, 1932)	1.12	.346
INNOVATION X SALARY	(14, 1946)	4.02	.0001
INNOVATION X YEARS	(28, 1981)	1.68	.01
PROGRAM EXPERIENCE	(1, 3026)	192.82	.0001
PROG. EXP. X INNOVATION	(7, 3026)	7.58	.0001
BETWEEN SUBJECTS			
GENDER	(1, 277)	.82	.36
RACE	(1, 276)	2.06	.152
YEARS WITH COMPANY	(4, 283)	.32	.86
SALARY GRADE	(2, 278)	4.59	.01

involving the scheduling of when employees are permitted to enter and leave the workplace.

EMPLOYEE BACKGROUND RESULTS

Researchers Inkeles and Smith have implied that acceptance of innovation in work organizations is related to an individual's life experiences as an employee:

... men become modern through the particular life experiences they undergo. ... employment in complex, rationalized, technocratic, and even bureaucratic organizations, has particular capabilities to change men so they move from the more traditional to the more modern pole in their attitudes, values and behavior. ... also ... age, religion, ethnic membership ... would be a good predictor of ... modernity.[13]

Thus it follows that an individual's organizational work relationships and demographic background might be related to acceptance of innovation.

Table 5.6 summarizes the means and standard deviations of acceptance by employee identity and organizational group memberships, which are discussed below in terms of the analysis of variance results. Two statistical tests were used to analyze significant differences between employee groups. For comparisons

Table 5.6
Means and Standard Deviations by Innovation and Employee Background
Variables (5 point scale: 1 strongly agree to 5 strongly disagree)

GENDER

INNOVATON	$\bar{x}$	Men sd	$\bar{x}$	Women sd
Flextime	1.89	.58	1.86	.58
Job Posting	2.55	.51	2.56	.52
Cash Award	3.04	.60	3.04	.56
Fitness Program	2.61	.59	2.51	.58
Flexible Benefits	3.32	.47	3.27	.45
Quality Circles	2.85	.64	2.86	.67
Newsletter	2.72	.58	2.60	.61
Peer Award	2.51	.64	2.70	.60

SALARY GRADE GROUP

INNOVATION	Officers $\bar{x}$	sd	Professionals $\bar{x}$	sd	Nonexempt $\bar{x}$	sd
Flextime	1.98	.58	1.83	.55	2.05	.67
Job Posting	2.47	.46	2.53	.51	2.70	.56
Cash Award	2.58	.64	3.11	.55	2.96	.54
Fitness Program	2.58	.66	2.58	.58	2.48	.56
Flexible Benefits	3.30	.53	3.31	.46	3.21	.41
Quality Circles	2.61	.67	2.86	.64	2.94	.65
Newsletter	2.73	.60	2.66	.61	2.56	.59
Peer Award	2.35	.49	2.66	.59	2.72	.67

RACE

INNOVATION	Caucasian $\bar{x}$	sd	Non-Caucasian $\bar{x}$	sd
Flextime	1.86	.58	2.06	.64
Job Posting	2.54	.52	2.67	.51
Cash Award	3.04	.58	2.99	.58
Fitness Program	2.57	.59	2.50	.53
Flexible Benefits	3.31	.46	3.18	.42
Quality Circles	2.85	.65	2.87	.55
Newsletter	2.63	.60	2.73	.65
Peer Award	2.61	.61	2.83	.65

Table 5.6 (continued)

ORGANIZATIONAL UNIT

INNOVATION	Data Processing		Financial Services	
	x̄	sd	x̄	sd
Flextime	1.85	.57	1.96	.61
Job Posting	2.54	.52	2.63	.52
Cash Award	3.05	.60	3.01	.53
Fitness Program	2.59	.59	2.46	.57
Flexible Benefits	3.31	.46	3.22	.45
Quality Circles	2.85	.64	2.87	.66
Newsletter	--	--	2.64	.60
Peer Award	--	--	2.64	.61

YEARS WITH COMPANY

INNOVATION	<1		1-5		6-10		11-15		≥16	
	x̄	sd	x̄	sd	x̄	sd	x̄	sd	x̄	sd
Flextime	1.72	.46	1.72	.51	1.92	.60	2.01	.59	2.08	.64
Job Posting	2.57	.41	2.51	.49	2.53	.54	2.59	.53	2.63	.56
Cash Award	2.98	.50	3.08	.53	3.11	.56	2.97	.61	2.99	.67
Fitness Program	2.68	.62	2.57	.60	2.55	.55	2.56	.60	2.52	.58
Flexible Benefits	3.21	.42	3.30	.47	3.28	.46	3.26	.47	3.36	.44
Quality Circles	2.93	.57	2.84	.67	2.88	.66	2.85	.63	2.82	.63
Newsletter	2.87	.45	2.54	.62	2.58	.62	2.72	.63	2.62	.60
Peer Award	2.68	.43	2.58	.64	2.63	.61	2.61	.68	2.70	.60

PROGRAM EXPERIENCE

INNOVATION	User		Nonuser	
	x̄	sd	x̄	sd
Flextime	1.79	.51	2.30	.72
Job Posting	2.47	.55	2.65	.47
Cash Award	2.62	.62	3.12	.54
Fitness Program	2.49	.56	3.01	.56
Flexible Benefits	2.60	.68	3.32	.43
Quality Circles	2.34	.73	2.99	.55
Newsletter	2.57	.59	3.11	.47
Peer Award	2.45	.65	2.75	.56

between two groups, t tests were used. Whenever it was necessary to make comparisons between more than two groups at the same time, the Student New-man-Keuls (SNK) statistic, a test of significant differences between all pairs of means, was used. Student Newman-Keuls uses the studentized range statistic and is appropriate for comparisons between samples of unequal sizes. With a small number of means, it is generally more conservative than repeated pairwise t tests in its outcomes and gives similar results to analyses using the Tukey honestly significant difference test.[14]

Hierarchical Level

For the analyses by hierarchical level (see Table 5.4), a multivariate analysis was conducted using a within-subjects design, which was significant ($F = 12.18$, $p < .0001$). In addition, hierarchical level was the only between-subjects variable that was significant ($F = 12.18$, $p < .0001$). Clearly, of all the background variables, hierarchical level was the most strongly related to acceptance of HRM innovation. The results show that officers and managers have the most favorable attitudes toward innovations aimed at lower level employees in which officers do not participate.

Officer and manager respondents, who comprised the highest hierarchical group, were the most accepting of quality circles, job posting, and recognition awards, which are all programs specifically targeted at nonexempt and profes-sional employees and excluded officers and managers by design (see Table 5.6). Officers and managers were significantly more accepting of quality circles than professionals and nonexempt employees ($SNK_{.05}$, 1625 df, critical value = .139). It is interesting that nonexempt employees rated the innovation poorly, because they are its heaviest users.

For job posting, officers and managers were the most favorable, followed closely by professionals. Nonexempt employees were substantially less accepting of job posting than higher level employees ($SNK_{.05}$, 1625 df, critical value = .111). The lower rating of job posting by nonexempt employees is particularly interesting if one considers that this innovation is probably the main vehicle available to help low level employees advance up the job ranks at VIC.

Officers and managers were by far the most accepting of the cash award program, followed by nonexempt and then professional employees ($SNK_{.05}$, 1625 df, critical value = .139). Data from group feedback interviews at VIC provided one explanation for the lower rating of the cash awards by professionals. Perhaps this group is the least favorable, because it includes most of the first level supervisors who have to deal with some of the negative day-to-day realities of administering the cash awards in their units, such as handling disgruntled non-recipients.

Of the innovations adopted only in Financial Services, significant differences were found between salary groups for the recognition award, but not for the employee newsletter. Officers were by far the most favorable group regarding the PAT award (SNK $_{.05}$, 278 df, critical value = .22). Professionals came next and were followed closely by nonexempt employees. A comparison of the officer's mean with that for nonofficers (professionals combined with nonexempts) was highly significant (t $_{52,308}$ = 3.77, p <.0002). Thus the findings for the peer award mirror the results for the cash award. Officers evidently like the idea of giving awards to subordinates. The high acceptance of People Are Tops by officers provides another example of an innovation that officers view favorably but do not directly use.

Although officers are eligible to be users of flextime, the fitness program, and flexible benefits, they were less favorable toward these innovations. An analysis of a significant interaction (F = 16.04, p < .0001) between innovation and hierarchical level indicated that officers and managers were significantly less favorable toward flextime and flexible benefits, which are innovations designed for the entire employee population. Professionals were more accepting of flextime than officers and nonexempts (SNK $_{.05}$, 1625 df, critical value = .139). Some employees interviewed suggested the lower rating by officers is probably because some officers believe that the innovation has resulted in a loss of productivity. The lower rating by nonexempt employees is perhaps because they have less freedom to actually use the innovation due to job constraints. For example, a receptionist must be at her desk for a very fixed time period, whereas a computer programmer has more flexibility in arranging the work schedule.

Flexible benefits was the only program that nonexempt employees were more accepting of than other employee groups (SNK $_{.05}$, 1625 df, critical value = .10). Data from feedback and review of company records indicate that these results may be a gender effect, as the vast majority of nonexempt positions were held by women who may be more interested in the innovation's day care advantages than men. Last, there were no significant differences by salary grade for the fitness program.

Gender and Racial Differences

Whereas there were no main effects for race or gender, significant interactions between race and innovation (F = 5.21, p < .0001) and gender and innovation (F = 2.45, p < .03) were found (see Table 5.4). These results suggest some variation in acceptance by race and gender for specific innovations.

As shown in Table 5.6, caucasian employees were significantly more accepting of flextime (t = 4.09, p < .0001) and job posting (t = 2.94, p < .003) than minority employees. However, minority employees were significantly more accepting of flexible benefits than caucasian workers (t = 3.13, p < .0018), which may be a hierarchical effect related to the concentration of minorities in nonexempt positions. Last, within Financial Services, nonwhite employees were significantly less accepting of the peer award than white employees (t$_{38,322}$, p > .0346), possibly because minority workers believe that they have less opportunity to receive the award.

The results for flextime and job posting may be intradepartmental effects. Minority employees' lower ratings for flextime appear to be due to the concentration of minorities in the data center in Data Processing and in a large marketing customer services unit. The data center was the only DP unit exempt from flextime, due to "business necessity" reasons. Similarly, the customer services unit had established work procedures in which clerical workers had to follow a planned flextime schedule that required them to work late on set days so that the work area is covered until 5 P.M., thereby restricting their use of the program. Similarly, these units were the least favorable in their respective departments regarding job posting, which supports feedback data indicating that career advancement opportunities are limited in these units.

The interaction between gender and innovation does not appear to be of importance. Whereas female employees were more accepting of the fitness program (t = 3.91, p < .0001) and flexible benefits (t = 2.28, p < .02) than male employees, men were not found to be significantly more accepting of any of the innovations. Within Financial Services, however, men were significantly more favorable than women regarding the peer award (t = 2.67, p < .008), and women were marginally more favorable (t = 1.79, p < .07) than men toward the newsletter. The People Are Tops findings are consistent with a significant difference ($t_{215,320}$ = 2.31, p < .022) occurring only within Financial Services for the cash awards, another innovation involving employee recognition, which showed men (2.92) were more favorable than women (3.06). One hypothesis that employees offered during feedback with the liaison group is that members of the largely female clerical population may believe they have less chance of being nominated for these awards.

Seniority

No main effect for years of service was found; however, a significant interaction between innovation and years of service was present (F = 4.14, p < .0001). The interaction was largely caused by the results for employees with less than one year of service. As shown in Table 5.6, new employees were highly favorable toward flextime ($SNK_{.05}$, 1551 df, critical value = .092) and flexible benefits ($SNK_{.05}$, 1419 df, critical value = .090) and are the least favorable toward the fitness program ($SNK_{.05}$, 1521 df, critical value = .087).

Data from group interviews indicated that flextime was useful in attracting employees to join the firm, and also showed that flexible benefits had been better communicated to new employees who had attended company orientation sessions during the past year than existing ones who had simply been mailed pamphlets. Interview data indicated that new employees' lower ratings for the fitness program stemmed from the rule that employees must have at least a year's service to be eligible to use the fitness center, despite new employees' eligibility to enjoy other program features upon joining the firm.

For Financial Services employees, a significant difference ($t_{29,340}$ = 2.18, p

< .03) was found by years of service for the newsletter. Employees with less than one year of service (2.87) were less favorable than all other groups (combined mean, 2.61). Discussion with the liaison group suggested that this may be due to new employees lack of familiarity with the *Grapevine*, as it had been discontinued during the reorganization and only one issue had gone out during the nine months prior to the survey.

Program Experience

For any analyses using the program experience variable, within and between subjects error terms were pooled in order to facilitate more accurate estimation.[15] Not surprisingly, users had much greater acceptance of all innovations than nonusers as in all cases (F = 605.84, p < .0001).

Table 5.4 shows one significant interaction with the program experience variable: innovation by program experience (F = 208.92, p < .0001). Users were more enthusiastic about some innovations than others. Whereas t tests that were conducted between the means for users and nonusers showed highly significant differences (p < .0001) for all of them, there was variation in the t value size. For example, the t value for quality circles t = 18.96, p < .0001) was a lot larger than the t value for job posting (t = 7.58, p < .0001).

Interview data indicated that the difference between participating in a quality circle and only hearing about it is probably greater than the difference between using job posting and only hearing about it. Participating in a circle is viewed as being a much more intense experience than filling out a job posting form to apply for a new position. Use of a quality circle involves the group experience of working with peers to solve an existing problem. In contrast, job posting is essentially an individual experience and many employees who post do not ever get chosen for a job interview.

Similarly, as shown in Table 5.6, nonusers of quality circles were much less enthusiastic than nonusers of job posting. Participants in group interviews stated that some nonparticipants thought that quality circle members thought they were "special" and superior to employees who weren't in the circle. For job posting, there is little of this intergroup rivalry between users and nonusers. For example, officers and managers were the most enthusiastic about job posting, despite their exclusion from using it.

Influence of Organizational Unit Membership

Although this study was conducted in only one organization, it was designed so that data could be collected from two different subunits of the firm. It was believed that differences in the way the innovation was implemented and in the demographic populations and organizational climates would influence the level of acceptance to innovation. The results supported these assumptions. There were differences in the way unit members responded to the innovations, not only between all employees in each unit, but also between only those who directly used the innovations.

The interaction (innovation $\times$ organizational unit) showed significant differences in acceptance for four of the six common innovations. Data Processing employees had significantly greater acceptance of flextime ($t_{483,1600} = 3.59$, p $< .0003$) and job posting ($t_{472,1576} = 3.35$, p $< .0008$), whereas Financial Services employees were more favorable on the Flexible Spending Account ($t_{404,1483} = 3.76$, p $< .0002$) and the fitness program ($t_{473,1576} = 4.37$, p $< .0001$).

Data Processing's greater acceptance of flextime is probably due, in part, to the unit's greater experimentation with forms of the innovation than Financial Services. Some employees interviewed said that unofficial flexible working hours were being followed by some managers to accommodate programmer preferences for unconventional working hours. Data Processing also had piloted an innovation allowing greater employee control over not only *when* they worked, but *where* they worked—work-at-home arrangements for new mothers. In contrast, when the top executive of Financial Services reviewed the questionnaire, he added the item, "Flextime has hurt the service level provided by my unit," and said some senior managers felt flextime has hurt productivity. Perhaps flextime is an innovation that is more congruent with work involving computers than work relating to marketing and serving customers, which might require more rigid hours of operation.

Data Processing's greater acceptance of job posting is also due to interunit differences in implementation. Data Processing maintains its own job posting program, which includes career counseling for its employees. It has tailored a corporate-initiated innovation to its needs. In Financial Services, however, a similar program was discontinued with the reorganization, which is missed by some employees; 41% of Financial Services respondents agreed with the item, "I wish we still had separate posting for Financial Services jobs like we used to have."

The greater acceptance of the Flexible Spending Account in Financial Services may be a gender effect. There are considerably more women in Financial Services than in Data Processing, and as the gender by innovation interaction discussed below shows, women were significantly more favorable on flexible benefits than men, presumably due to the day care benefits it offers. Data from interviews suggest that Financial Services' greater acceptance of the fitness program than Data Processing is probably due to the fact that the innovation can be marketed to customers. This feature holds greater immediate interest for marketing personnel than Data Processing personnel.

If interunit differences in the acceptance existed for all employees, it makes sense that there were interunit differences for the actual users of the innovations. The user by organizational unit interaction and user by organizational unit by innovation triple interaction were caused by flextime, job posting, the fitness program, and quality circles. These results can be attributed to differences in the extent to which the benefits offered by the innovations met the needs of unit members.

Data Processing users had significantly greater acceptance ($t_{120,249}$ = 6.34, p < .0001) of quality circles than Financial Services users, which was the largest interunit difference for users. These results are not surprising given the differences in the overall health and current life-cycle stages of the quality circle programs. With a decreasing number of circles in operation, Financial Services' program is on the demise, whereas Data Processing's program is still expanding. Whereas most of Financial Services' circles involved clerical workers, Data Processing's circles included college-educated technical professionals and even some middle managers. Management support for the circles is also a greater problem for Financial Services. Although nearly half (47%) of Financial Services respondents agreed with the item, "It would be good if more officers and managers participated in Innovation Through Involvement," only a third (34%) of Data Processing's respondents did so.

Data Processing's users of flextime and the job posting program were also significantly more accepting of these innovations than Financial Services' users of these programs (flextime: $t_{350,1310}$ = 4.29; job posting: $t_{202,823}$ = 3.75, p < .0002). However, Financial Services' users were more significantly favorable toward the fitness program ($t_{352,1336}$ = 3.68, p < .0002) than Data Processing's users. These differences can be all attributed to the interunit differences in implementation described above.

Summary of Effects of Employee Background on Acceptance

In summary, of all background variables, hierarchical level was most closely related to acceptance of innovation. Officers and managers were the most accepting of quality circles, job posting, and employee awards, which are all innovations aimed at low level employees. These innovations are designed to enhance productivity and address senior management's need to take action to improve the profitability of the firm. Unfortunately, lower level employees do not share management's enthusiasm for these programs.

THE SOCIAL PROPERTIES OF INNOVATIONS

A key assumption of the study described in this book is that there are common social properties of human resource innovations that can be used to analyze their impact on employees. In order to investigate how the characteristics of the innovations influence acceptance, several months after the study had been completed, an impartial panel of experts in human resource management who worked for large corporations reviewed the features of the innovations in order to shed additional light on the results.

The four experts rated descriptions of the eight innovations along five dimensions using a five-point Likert-type scale (1 low to 5 high). These dimensions

Table 5.7
Reliabilities and Interrater Agreement Correlations for Four Experts' Ratings of Innovations

Dimension	Mean Intercorrelation	Reliability*
Performance Impact	.70	.90
Empowerment	.70	.90
Intensity	.40	.73
Frequency	.54	.82
Intrusiveness	.02	.06

*Spearman-Brown coefficient

all involved social properties of the innovations that the researcher believed had an important influence on acceptance. These variables, which were selected on the basis of knowledge gained by the researcher during the study are: (1) performance impact, the extent to which this innovation will positively affect an employee's performance on the job, (2) degree of empowerment, the extent to which this innovation will give an employee greater control over his/her job, (3) intensity, the intensity of impact this innovation will have on an employee's attitudes or behavior, (4) frequency, the relative frequency of times an employee will probably come in contact with the innovation, and (5) intrusiveness, the extent to which this innovation will intrude on an employee's day-to-day work environment on the job. It was believed that all of these variables would be positively related to acceptance.

A mean interrater correlation and Spearman-Brown reliability coefficient were computed for each dimension, shown in Table 5.7. The average interjudge agreement and reliabilities for each dimension were reasonably high for all of the properties except intrusiveness, which was dropped from the analysis.

Table 5.8 shows the means and standard deviations for the panel of experts' ratings of the innovations on the four dimensions. It is interesting to note that flextime, the innovation with the greatest acceptance, ranks first for intensity and frequency, second for empowerment, and third for performance impact. Although the quality circles studied at VIC were not overwhelmingly accepted by employees, the panel of experts also rated them quite favorably. Quality circles ranked first for performance impact and empowerment, second for intensity, but fifth for frequency. Whereas these results could be spurious because of the small number of experts who rated the innovations, they suggest high

Table 5.8
Means and Standard Deviations for the Panel of Experts' Ratings of the Innovations

1 (LOW) TO 5 (HIGH) SCALE

Innovation	Empowerment		Intensity		Frequency		Performance Impact	
	x̄	sd	x̄	sd	x̄	sd	x̄	sd
Job Posting	2.30	1.19	3.44	.82	3.52	1.17	1.63	.43
Quality Circles	4.67	.52	4.15	1.44	3.16	1.60	3.95	.74
Flextime	4.02	1.39	4.20	.91	4.94	.12	3.22	.68
Fitness Program	1.25	.38	2.83	1.28	2.65	.55	2.30	.87
Cash Award	1.46	.49	3.43	1.26	2.02	.78	3.20	.91
Flexible Benefits	1.30	.48	2.57	.99	4.15	.87	1.18	.38
Peer Recognition	1.80	.91	3.60	1.14	2.92	.94	3.70	.81
Newsletter	2.10	1.04	2.30	.94	3.35	.52	1.35	.45

intensity and frequency may be useful dimensions to consider, in addition to an employee's level in the organization, when studying acceptance. It is also interesting to observe that high performance impact may not be the most important property that influences high acceptance.

The results of a correlation matrix of the relationships between the innovations' characteristics and their acceptance are found in Table 5.9. In addition to the four dimensions rated by the experts, the matrix includes the following for each innovation: age in months, rate of employee participation as a portion of total unit population, and logarithm of annual dollars spent, since there was a wide range in the amount of money allocated to the programs. Because the amount of dollars spent on the innovations, innovation age, and participation rates differed by unit, the correlations are broken down by unit, which show very similar results.

The variable of innovation age was included in the analysis because it was believed that acceptance would vary over time. Innovations that are very new may have low acceptance, because of lack of employee awareness of and familiarity with them. Innovations that are very old may also have low acceptance

Table 5.9

Correlations of Innovation Characteristics and Acceptance by Organizational Unit

Data Processing: N = 6 INNOVATIONS

	1.	2.	3.	4.	5.	6.	7.	8.
1.ACCEPTANCE	-							
DIMENSIONS								
2.EMPOWERMENT	.50	-						
3.FREQUENCY	.49	.42	-					
4.INTENSITY	.60	.91***	.24	-				
5.PERFORMANCE IMPACT	.30	.70	.21	.81**	-			
6.AGE (MONTHS)	.34	.17	.17	.21	-.25	-		
7.PARTICIPATION RATE	.88**	.13	.26	.22	.12	.14	-	
8.LOGARITHM OF DOLLARS	.60	-.68	-.62	-.75*	-.27	-.53	-.16	-

Financial Services: N = 8 INNOVATIONS

	1.	2.	3.	4.	5.	6.	7.	8.
1.ACCEPTANCE	-							
DIMENSIONS								
2.EMPOWERMENT	.38	-						
3.FREQUENCY	.43	.43	-					
4.INTENSITY	.39	.75**	.17	-				
5.PERFORMANCE IMPACT	.22	.53	-.24	.83***	-			
6.AGE (MONTHS)	.22	.25	.19	.22	-.22	-		
7.PARTICIPATION RATE	.86****	.25	.27	-.01	-.02	.05	-	
8.LOGARITHM OF DOLLARS	.38	-.55	-.38	-.54	-.33	-.36	-.12	-

* P < .1; ** P < .05; *** P < .01; **** P < .006

as employees are all too familiar with them, and their design may have become out of sync with employee needs. Money was thought to be an important variable, because it is an indicator of the level of formal organizational support given to the innovation. Participation rates were thought to be positively related to acceptance. If an innovation is used by many employees, perhaps it will receive high acceptance, because it appears to be an integral program.

Of the eight dimensions, only one, the participation rate, was significantly positively related to acceptance. However, these results can be misleading because they are based on a small number of ratings. Rather than the participation rate, conceptually, it may be more fruitful to conduct future study of the influence of the innovations' intensity, degree of empowerment, financial support, and frequency of usage on acceptance. Although not significant, these variables had moderately strong positive correlations with acceptance.

Last, it is useful to examine the correlations among the dimensions. Intensity was significantly correlated with empowerment and performance impact, but marginally negatively correlated with the amount of financial support spent on the innovations. The latter correlation suggests that innovations with high intensity may not necessarily cost a lot in financial terms.

NOTES

1. A. Tsui, and G. Milkovich, "Personnel Department Activities: Constituency Perspectives and Preferences," *Personnel Psychology* 40 (1987), 519–537.

2. See, e.g., H. Gorlin, and L. Schein, *Innovations in Managing Human Resources*, New York: Conference Board (1984), and L. R. Gomez, and D. B. Balkin, "Dimensions and Characteristics of Personnel Managers Perceptions of Effective Drug-Testing Programs," *Personnel Psychology* 40, no. 4 (1987), 745–764.

3. See, e.g., A. S. Tsui, "Defining the Activities and Effectiveness of the Human Resource Department: A Multiple Constituency Approach," *Human Resource Management* 26, no. 1 (1987): 35–69, and Gomez and Balkin, "Dimensions and Characteristics."

4. G. R. Ungson, and R. M. Steers, "Motivation and Politics in Executive Compensation," *Academy of Management Review* 9 (1984): 313–323.

5. See, e.g., R. A. Noe, and N. Schmitt, "The Influence of Trainees Attitudes on Training Effectiveness: Test of a Model," *Personnel Psychology* 39 (1986).

6. C. J. Berger, and L. L. Cummings, "Organizational Structure, Attitudes, and Behaviors," *Research in Organizational Behavior* 1 (1979), 169–208.

7. Tsui and Milkovich, "Personnel Department Activities."

8. See, e.g., M. K. Mount, "Comparisons of Managerial and Employee Satisfaction with a Performance Appraisal System," *Personnel Psychology* 36 (1983), 99–110, or E. E. Lawler, A. M. Mohrman, and S. M. Resnick, "Performance Appraisal Revisited," *Organizational Dynamics* 13 (1983), 20–35.

9. See, e.g., C. Daly and S. Hammond, "Work Orientation as a Function of Sex, Job Level and Marital Status," *Irish Journal of Psychology* 6, no. 2 (1984): 146–155; E. A. Fagenson, "Women's Work Orientations: Something Old, Something New," *Group and Organization Studies* 11, no. 1–2 (1984): 75–100; and P. E. Varca, G. S. Shaffer, and C. D. McCauley, "Sex Differences in Job Satisfaction Revisited," *Academy of Management Journal* 26, no. 2 (1983): 348–353.

10. See, e.g., J. P. Fernandez, *Racism and Sexism in Corporate Life* (New York: Lexington, 1981); R. M. Kanter, *Men and Women of the Corporation* (New York: Basic

Books, 1977); and R. M. Kanter, *The Changemasters* (New York: Simon and Schuster, 1983).

11. G. Bocialetti, "Quality of Work Life: Some Unintended Effects on the Seniority Tradition of an Industrial union," *Group and Organization Studies* 12 (1987), 386–410.

12. E. E. Ghiselli, J. P. Campbell, and S. Zedeck, *Measurement Theory for the Behavioral Sciences* (New York: W. H. Freeman, 1981), 256.

13. A. Inkeles, and D. Smith, *Becoming Modern: Individual Change in Six Developing Countries* (Cambridge, Mass.: Harvard University Press, 1974).

14. B. J. Winer, *Statistical Principles in Organizational Design*, 2nd ed. (New York: McGraw-Hill, 1971), 216–218.

15. B. F. Green, and J. W. Tukey, "Complex Analyses of Variance: General Problems," *Psychometrika* 25 (1960): 127–152.

6

Lessons for Managers of Human Resource Innovations

This chapter includes a discussion of some of the lessons that VIC's experience with HRM innovations offers for managers of personnel programs in organizations. The track record for HRM innovations at VIC is probably similar to that of many other departments. An examination of what worked well and not so well at VIC offers insight into the difficulties of successfully managing HRM innovations.

TEN HRM LESSONS

1. *Many human resource innovators are not market-oriented in designing new programs.*

Whereas line managers at VIC often thought and behaved in terms of how they believed key markets would respond, human resource managers tended not to act in terms of markets, a concept embedded in the line management ethos. Many of the innovations adopted at VIC were designed with limited input from the employees who had to use them. The needs and desires of employees were not the prime consideration in the initiation of innovation. For example, employees certainly didn't ask for quality circles or flexible benefits, and the way these programs were designed did not seem to benefit their interests. Employees were generally not viewed as the primary clientele of HRM initiatives. Clearly, the issues of "who are the clients?" or "who do these new programs serve?" are raised.

The HRM innovators at VIC seemed more concerned with external market forces rather than internal ones. Programs such as quality circles, cash awards, or job posting were initiated in order to either mimic leading competitors or to respond to coercive pressures like government regulation. Sometimes the innovators simply viewed employees as their own guinea pigs in a corporate laboratory as in the case of the fitness program. Whereas none of these rationale for adoption are necessarily "bad" in and of themselves, the appalling fact remains that little, if any, internal market research was done prior to the adoption of any of VIC's programs.

2. *Developing meaningful avenues that allow for greater employee participation in the design and implementation of new programs is beneficial for the long-term acceptance of HRM innovations.*

In their study on implementing organizational innovations, W. R. Nord and S. Tucker identified three key ingredients for "successful implementation": listening to staff, flexibility, and access to technical competence.[1] Applying these concepts to HRM innovations, successful personnel initiatives must be adopted and implemented in accordance with employee needs and desires. These innovations should be open to modifications in their design and operation based on the reactions of product users, the group that is the most technically competent to assess their relative merits.

The low acceptance of many of the innovations at VIC emphasize the critical need to obtain local line management and employee involvement in the design and implementation of new programs. For example, whereas employees might like the idea of having flexibility in their benefits package or having the opportunity to receive a cash bonus for outstanding performance "in concept," their dislike of the way that the programs were designed and implemented nullified any of the potential for positively influencing employee behavior. Had the human resource department allowed for greater participation in the design and implementation of these programs, it is likely that the initiatives would have been a lot more successful.

Conducting employee focus groups and surveys prior and after adoption are just a few of the steps companies can take to facilitate acceptance. Once input is gotten, however, it is critical that HRM managers act on the information and incorporate the input into the administration of the programs. Such an approach necessitates having an implementation plan that allows for flexibility in program design so that minor modifications can be made during implementation.

Because of the obvious ramifications that a human resource innovation has on the social system, it appears that participation of employees and line management in the decision to adopt and implement the innovation is crucial for acceptance. Participation should not only increase local ownership, but will hopefully result in better designed innovations that more closely reflect employee interests.

3. *The stature of the Human Resources department in the organization affects the degree to which the communication of innovations is successful.*

Despite the attempts to publicize human resource innovations through such means as company newspapers and flyers sent home, employee awareness of some human resource innovations such as flexible benefits and the cash awards was extremely low. For example, 76% of the respondents agreed with the statement, ''I am familiar with the main features of job posting,'' and 77% agreed that they were familiar with the fitness program. In contrast, only 48% were familiar with the main features of flexible benefits and only 45% were familiar with cash awards. Perhaps if the communication efforts had been done interpersonally by a peer or a first line supervisor, employees might have been more aware of flexible benefits and cash awards, innovations with low frequency and intensity.

But perhaps even more importantly, employees' perceptions of the formal owner of the innovation, the Human Resource department, probably had something to do with the relative ineffectiveness of VIC's communication efforts. Clearly, the results from the work environment section suggest that of the three groups, top management, immediate supervisors, and the Human Resources department, employees had the least favorable attitudes toward Human Resources. Oskamp has shown that the credibility and attractiveness of the communicator can influence attitudes toward new work programs.[2] The key to gaining acceptance of work innovations may be to give supervisors the primary role in communicating them. The success of using such an approach, however, assumes that a firm is promoting capable individuals and training them well in supervisory and human resources practices. Certainly, the training of supervisors in the communication of the introduction of flextime and job posting appeared to have a positive influence on their acceptance at VIC.

In addition, HRM departments might take steps to improve their internal company image as one means of facilitating acceptance of the work innovations they manage. Taking steps to improve the perceived credibility, trustworthiness, and effectiveness of the HRM unit may have a more powerful effect on the extent to which programs are successful than any other action that might be taken. If the personnel department is respected, it is likely that its programs will be viewed accordingly.

4. *Organizations tend to place the least emphasis on evaluation in the human resource adoption process.*

In adopting new programs, VIC's primary organizational focus was on design, not evaluation. Once approval for adopting an innovation was gotten, and the innovation had been introduced, little follow-up scrutiny was conducted. Organizations seem to emphasize *quantity* of HRM innovation over the *quality*. It would be desirable for more managers (and researchers and consultants) to recognize that evaluation of human resource innovation is a separate activity from design and initiation, and make it an organizational priority.

Unfortunately, an emphasis on evaluation, which requires long-term top management attention, simply does not exist for many Human Resource programs. Other than the fitness program, the innovation that was likely to be marketed to customers and eventually influence corporate sales and profitability, little formal evaluation had been conducted on the innovations. The managers seemed to be content to rely on anecdotal evidence and individual testimony regarding the effectiveness of innovations. Assessment of HRM innovations' impact on productivity and employee attitudes will not only provide useful data on how to improve the administration of the innovations, but also will help the HRM department in getting top management support for future HRM efforts. The demonstration that HRM initiatives can favorably influence the bottom line will certainly enhance the likelihood that line management will approve the allocation of additional resources to HRM programs.

5. *Innovations that are well administered and designed to be an integral part of the work system require less proselytism than poorly administered, peripheral innovations.*

As the Corporate Personnel executive who managed the introduction of the fitness program exclaimed in an interview, ''You've got to keep it out in front of them all the time.'' Clearly, the results of the study show that the need for human resource managers to push new programs on employees is greater for some innovations than others. Innovations such as flextime truly offered employees tangible benefits, whereas others such as quality circles appeared to offer more fluff than substance. Unlike Innovation Through Involvement, flextime wasn't a separate program that was peripheral to the day-to-day work environment. Rather, it involved the daily managing of employee behavior on the job. Whereas flextime influenced the nature of the supervisor and employee interaction every day, quality circles had infrequent influence if any and were viewed as being removed from employees' ''regular work.'' Innovations may be more likely to receive acceptance if they are designed to be an important element of the work environment. Also, it is unlikely that such well-designed innovations would have to be pushed by personnel.

6. *Human Resource innovations that are clearly related to the main goals of the firm will receive the largest financial support.*

Of all of the innovations studied, VIC spent by far the greatest amount of money on the fitness program. This innovation, which was invented by a marketing unit for use in increasing customer sales, is the human resource program that was closest to VIC's main business, insurance. If more and more client organizations can persuade their employees to lead healthier lives, then VIC would pay out lower benefits on policies. The concept of ''where's the laboratory?'' was offered by the corporate fitness program sponsor to top management as a method of gaining support for the adoption of a major human resource management innovation. Perhaps top management was persuaded to allow such an ambitious internal change to be adopted because of the tangible economic benefits that the fitness program had the potential to offer.

VIC spent the next largest amount of money on flexible benefits, another innovation in the health care cost containment arena. As the following comments by one employee regarding his use of flexible benefits indicates, the tangible benefits of some of these trial balloons can fail to trickle down to employees. He stated, "I think VIC should stop experimenting on their employees with financial packages before they have adequately trained their people and gotten the bugs out of the system. They had no problem taking the money out of my paycheck immediately, but in order to get my check I had to badger them with phone calls and personal visits. There was a problem with entering my claim into the system and nobody was particularly motivated to fix it."

7. *Local personnel units should be given as much opportunity as possible to administer the innovation in a way that meets local needs. Avoid uniformity in implementation for uniformity's sake.*

In today's current business environment of mega-mergers and the growing employee size of many Fortune companies, one might believe that centralized implementation of uniformly designed personnel programs would be an appropriate human resource strategy. However, the results of this study clearly suggest taking the opposite approach. It is apparent that high congruence between the *benefits* provided by the innovation and the particular needs of the local population is necessary for high acceptance. Hence, acceptance is not dependent on the extent of congruence between innovation's *design* and the relevant needs of the local population, but rather on the extent to which the benefits offered by the innovation's *implementation* are congruent with the needs of unit members.

In all instances, the significant interunit differences in acceptance that were found can be attributed to differences in the extent to which the innovation's benefits met the needs of local members. Consider the differences in acceptance between members of Financial Services and Data Processing. Flextime and job posting were significantly more accepted in Data Processing, and the fitness program and flexible benefits were significantly more accepted in Financial Services. Whereas Financial Services relied totally on the corporate system, job posting had been tailored to meet local needs in Data Processing, which maintained its own posting system giving internal candidates not only first dibs on openings, but also career counseling.

Similarly, recall the key differences in the implementation of flexible working arrangements between the units. Data Processing had formally piloted a work-at-home program for working mothers and informally overlooked some managers apparent disregard for the core corporate hours by signing time cards of employees (often programmers) who had worked unconventional hours. Similarly, Financial Services users were more enthusiastic about Taking Care, because the program was clearly tailored to meet its local business needs of selling to and servicing customers. Last, the day care provision of flexible benefits ostensibly met the needs of the many female members of Financial Services, whereas Data Processing, in contrast, had a much smaller female population.

8. *Many HRM innovations are likely to fail, because line management and worker ownership of most human resource advances is limited. Unfortunately, employee and management ownership is critical to success.*

Despite efforts to involve line management, ownership for all the innovations in this study were viewed by the organization at large to rest with the personnel department, which sometimes placed it in an adversarial and proselytizing role. As one marketing group line manager said, "I tend to have concern about some programs that are introduced, but are all too soon forgotten. The minute top management stops being identified with them, the programs end up having personnel people trying to push them."

This staff-line conflict has historical roots, as Personnel departments often were first formed to control and centralize the employee-organization relationship.[3] An adversarial relationship between personnel and line management can lock an organization into a human resource innovation-resisting pattern. A tension that often cannot be resolved is how to gain line ownership for human resource innovations that are the purview of professionals who have generally lacked empowerment as a group in many firms and have had limited work experience in the core business functions. Consequently, personnel managers often do not possess all the competencies that their positions require in order to do their jobs well. As a result, they can develop a kind of passive-aggressive, withdrawing and comprising relationship to line management.

Line management, on the other hand, often has a highly possessive hierarchical view of authority (especially their own), because of their position of power in the firm. They can undermine Human Resource's efforts to be effective and can make sure that no competent Human Resources executive ever gets enough line management access or authority to make a difference. Thus the two groups get locked into an innovation-resisting pattern.

Issues of control and the historical staff-line conflict are key outcomes emanating from the less than overwhelming acceptance of many personnel innovations at VIC. When human resource innovations fail, it is because they are viewed as intruding upon local line management authority and subtlely competing with the firm's formal authority structure, are viewed as separate programs, or are poorly designed and administered. Although the Human Resource professionals might view the innovations as worthwhile, various employees and groups may not hold the same opinion, particularly if the innovators have not had a lot of interaction with other members in designing and implementing them.

Analyses of the level of acceptance to the six innovations adopted in Data Processing, for example, found key differences in the level of acceptance between members of the Human Resources division and all other employees for three of the programs. Human Resources was significantly more accepting of the cash awards and the fitness program than all other employees. Human Resources mean for cash awards was 2.82, whereas members of other divisions ranked it unfavorably 3.07 ($t_{128,1403} = 4.65$, $p < .0001$). Cash awards were designed totally by members of Human Resources. In addition, nearly all of the members of the committee in Data Processing that reviews the awards are members of Human Resources.

Similarly, HR managers were significantly more accepting of the fitness program than other employee groups. For the fitness program, which was managed by a long-time member of Human Resources, the Human Resources mean was 2.40, whereas the combined mean for all other divisions was 2.61, a significant difference ($t_{131,1435} = 4.03$, p < .0001). In contrast, members of Human Resources were significantly less favorable regarding flextime (1.96) than those in all other divisions (1.84) ($t_{133,1466} = 2.26$, p <.02). Whereas flextime was by far the most preferred innovation of line employees in Data Processing, perhaps Personnel was less enthusiastic because its members have to manage some of the day-to-day headaches of its administration like collecting and checking employee time sheets.

9. *An examination of the history of adoption of a sample of human resource programs at a firm can give insight into a company's human resource innovation philosophy.*

VIC's history with the eight innovations provided insight into its overall approach to the adoption and implementation of new people practices. The innovations, in effect, served as landmarks on VIC's organizational map of human resource management. J. Kimberly[4] points out that there are two types of organizations: inventors of innovations and consumers of innovations. With the exception of the *Grapevine*, VIC clearly leaned toward the consumer of innovation typology, which has obvious ramifications for acceptance. Whereas innovations that have been proven in another terrain may have greater chances for adoption than those invented internally, they may not necessarily receive high acceptance, particularly if the benefits they provide are incongruent with employee needs. As the data on the generally low level of top management support given to the innovations also indicate, VIC officers may value human resource innovation to a lesser extent than their counterparts in organizations characterized as inventors of innovation.

Within VIC, there were also subcultures regarding human resource innovation. Local management interest appeared to be a key factor differentiating the initiation of innovation between units. Data Processing management was fairly innovative regarding their implementation of flextime and job posting. These efforts paid off, as evinced by the significantly greater acceptance of these innovations by both the general Data Processing population and users than in Financial Services.

In contrast, Financial Services management was innovative in the adoption of People Are Tops and the *Grapevine*, programs that do not even exist in Data Processing. Perhaps the reason why these innovations received only lukewarm acceptance (with a mean score of 2.64 for People Are Tops and 2.63 for the newsletter, they ranked lower than flextime, the fitness program, and job posting) is because members have seen a lot of personnel programs tried and then subsequently discontinued. Evidence for this is provided by responses to an item in the work environment section of the questionnaire. Over a third (38%) of the respondents in Financial Services agreed with the statement, "A lot of personnel programs come and go around here," in contrast to 28% for Data Processing. There are several examples of the fickleness of Financial Services regarding HRM innovation. Financial Services had a precursor to quality circles, Productivity Through Job Involvement, that was dropped when Innovation Through Involvement was initiated. The *Grapevine* was initially discontinued after the reorganization and then resurrected several months later. Although Financial Services used to have a separate job posting program that gave its employees first dibs on vacancies, the program was dropped when the department was reorganized. Certainly, the unit appears to lack perseverance regarding HRM initiatives.

10. *The dynamics of corporate and local personnel departments (i.e., politics) has an important influence on the adoption and acceptance of human resource innovation.*

As R. Walton[5] noted in his classic study on the Topeka project, some of the difficulties in achieving long-term success for an innovation can be attributed to political problems between corporate and local actors. The current study also suggests that successfully managing the tension between local and corporate ownership of human resource innovations may be critical to the effectiveness of the innovations.

For a variety of reasons such as greater resources and access to top management, it is likely that corporate human resource departments will initiate a greater number of HRM innovations than local departments, which are often engaged in the day-to-day realities of administering personnel programs. A key ingredient for gaining local ownership for corporate programs is the managing of the adoption of the innovation in a true partnership with local personnel managers. At VIC, for example, some of the innovations that Corporate Personnel introduced were relatively more accepted (flextime, job posting) than others (flexible spending account, cash awards). The difference may be partly attributed to the extent to which open meetings were held to allow the local managers to have input into the design of the innovations, as well as involvement with the mechanics of implementation. The poor *designs* of flexible benefits and cash awards in terms of a low fit between their features and the needs of employees and the *ways* in which they were introduced (with little or no initial local input) limited their acceptance.

NOTES

1. W. R. Nord, and S. Tucker, *Implementing Routine and Radical Innovations* (Lexington, Mass.: D. C. Heath, 1987), 300–317.

2. S. Oskamp, *Attitudes and Opinions* (Englewood-Cliff, N.J.: Prentice-Hall, 1977).

3. T. Kochan, and P. Cappelli, "The Transformation of the Industrial Relations and the Personnel Function," in P. Osterman, ed., *Internal Labor Markets* (Cambridge, Mass.: MIT Press, 1984), 133–161.

4. J. Kimberly, "Managerial Innovation," in P. Nystrom and W. Starbuck, eds., *Handbook of Organizational Design* (Oxford: Oxford University Press, 1981), 84–104.

5. R. Walton, "The Diffusion of New Work Structures: Explaining Why Success Didn't Take," *Organizational Dynamics* (1975), 3–22.

7
Conclusions

The objectives of the study described in this book were to examine the behavioral and attitudinal consequences of eight human resource management innovations in a single corporation called VIC. Specifically, the purpose of the study was to understand the relationship between employee hierarchical level and other background characteristics (race, sex, seniority, program experience, organizational unit) and acceptance of human resource management (HRM) innovation. The goal of the research was to extend our understanding of HRM innovations by examining acceptance of multiple innovations across organizational hierarchical levels using attitudinal and self-reported behavioral measures.

A questionnaire on attitudes toward eight HRM programs was collected from 2018 employees in one firm. The programs studied included: quality circles, flextime, flexible benefits, job posting, cash awards, a fitness program, an employee-run newsletter, and a peer award. Using a within-subjects design, the results from analyses of variance indicated that (1) executives and managers accept HRM innovations more than nonmanagement employees, particularly those that are designed for nonmanagers, and (2) innovations that improve the quality of life of many members receive high acceptance. The findings imply that previous research on acceptance of innovative HRM programs may tend to overstate their effectiveness. In this chapter, rationales for these findings are discussed as well as research implications that focus on the need to shape HRM innovations to better reflect employee preferences. Prior to discussing these issues, however, it is insightful to consider the influence of VIC's unique organizational culture of human resource management on the results.

HUMAN RESOURCE INNOVATION AT VIC

The following remark made by a Data Processing employee in an interview gives insight into the attitudes of many employees regarding human resource management innovation at VIC: "A lot of these programs were started so that the senior vice president can say to his boss or the chairman can say to the board of directors, 'Look at all the money I've spent on my employees. I have to be doin' a good job.' It's not clear to me that it ever goes any deeper than that. Maybe it's a marketing approach. We talked about followup and commitment to quality circles . . . great program then pssst, it just sorta fizzled out. Most of the technocrats that work here could care less about these programs."

As this employee's remarks imply, many human resource innovations adopted by management have little positive impact on workers' lives.

Similarly, other employees have suggested in interviews or on their surveys that these programs are really perceived as Band-Aids to cover up weaknesses in basic company benefits and compensation. Some employees believe that innovations are introduced in order to mask shortcomings related to the amount of remuneration VIC gives to its workers. They view the innovations as a psychological means of controlling employee attitudes toward the employer, HRM innovations implemented to pacify employee discontent over deficiencies in basic company benefits and pay levels.

Other employees view human resource innovations as peripheral to their "real" day-to-day work. As one respondent wrote, "Participation in programs should be somewhat limited—i.e., if an employee is involved in too many programs it results in time away from his/her desk involving other employees answering his/her phone, which means time away from their own job."

Clearly, there is a lot of room for improvement in VIC's track record of human resource management innovation. Data from employee responses to questionnaire items about personnel innovation at VIC back this up. For example, only 21% of the respondents agreed with the statement, "Most of the personnel programs that are tried in my division are successful." Only 14% of the respondents disagreed with the statement, "A lot of personnel programs come and go around here." Less than half of the respondents (48%) agreed with the statement, "My supervisor usually backs new human resources programs." In general, the perceived performance of HRM innovations attempted at VIC is less than stellar, to say the least.

Not surprisingly, employees at VIC hold the Human Resources department in low esteem, which is the chief communicator and owner of personnel innovations. It is useful to recall respondents' mean favorability ratings for three key groups in the firm: top management, supervisors, and Human Resources. Supervisors were rated the most favorably (2.45), top management came next (2.56), and the Human Resources department was viewed the least favorably (2.74). Even with a mean of 2.45, employees are not overwhelmingly enthusiastic regarding their supervisors, which alludes to the poor organizational climate at VIC.

For example, less than half of the respondents (46%) agreed with the item, "People in my division trust each other." Only 43% of the respondents agreed with the item, "Sufficient effort is made to get the opinions and thinking of people who work here." Just over half of the respondents (55%) agreed with the statement, "In general, communications in my unit are good." Similarly, a bare majority (51%) of the respondents agreed with the statement, "The decisions management make in my department are usually fair." A little over half of the respondents (52%) agreed with the statement, "Most of the time it's safe to say what you think around here." Only 42% of responding employees agreed with the item, "In general, the reporting structure in my area will remain constant in the future."

The results for acceptance of innovation are unequivocally going to be influenced by the culture of human resource management innovation at VIC, as well as the existing malaise of the organizational climate. Perhaps many VIC members resist accepting new personnel programs, because many of the innovations do little to improve the overall quality of life of most employees. Despite this preceding discussion of the unique context for studying human resource innovation at VIC, however, it is not suggested that the results are not generalizable. There are undoubtedly many organizations in corporate and public America that have a human resource innovation climate that is similar to the one at VIC. Thus the results are the most appropriately applied to firms with attributes that predispose members to be human resource innovation-resisting.

HIERARCHICAL DIFFERENCES IN ACCEPTANCE OF INNOVATION

The results clearly show that hierarchical level is positively related to attitudes toward HRM innovations. Officers and managers, the highest level employees, tended to accept HRM innovations more favorably than lower level employees, particularly those programs that were specifically targeted at nonmanagers such as quality circles, job posting, and employee recognition awards. Ironically, these are all innovations that senior employees don't directly use. Overall, hierarchical level was by far more strongly related to acceptance of HRM innovation than race, gender, or seniority, which is consistent with previous research findings showing that hierarchical level is a good predictor of favorable workplace attitudes.

Several explanations can be made for these results. They are: (1) senior employees receive greater benefits from personnel innovations than lower and middle level employees, (2) senior employees participated in the decision to adopt the innovations, unlike members of lower hierarchical groups, and (3) senior employees have a halo effect in regards to attitudes toward the workplace: they tend to be enthusiastic about aspects of their employment, in general.

The Intangible Benefits of HRM Innovation

Perhaps the *intangible benefits* that officers and managers derive from HRM innovations are greater than the tangible benefits afforded middle and lower level employees. HRM innovations may help give the impression that management leads a firm with competitive state-of-the art programs and may also help validate the legitimacy of the personnel system among management. By initiating HR programs and allocating considerable dollars to personnel activities, executives can ostensibly demonstrate their interest in the employee population to the chairman and board of directors, the community, competitors, and the workers themselves.

Perhaps human resource management programs serve a symbolic role: they provide evidence that top management acts as if it cares about its employees. They also give the impression that executives lead a firm with competitive personnel programs and validate the legitimacy of the human resource system among top management. Certainly this symbolic view of HRM innovations is consistent with L. Smircich's and C. Stubbart's[1] contention that the primary role of management is the management of meaning. In order to serve this role, officers and managers may develop a pro-innovation bias toward the latest fads, perhaps placing an overemphasis on the quantity of HRM innovation as opposed to quality. Despite managers' and officers' favorable ratings of programs designed for subordinates, the results suggest that lower level employees may view these programs as having more fluff than substance. Nonexempt and professional employees' relatively lower ratings suggest that many of the supposed main constituents of the programs don't necessarily want them or like them, or at best are ambivalent toward them.

For example, only 5% of Financial Services respondents agreed with the statement, "The People Are Tops award is very important to me." Only 17% of responding employees agreed that quality circles were very important to them. Only 21% of the respondents agreed with the statement, "The Outstanding Achievement award is very important to me." Less than half of the respondents (45%) agreed that job posting was very important to them. Indeed, less than half of the responding employees were convinced that the management was sincerely interested in its employees. Only 43% agreed with the statement, "Financial Services (or Data Processing) top management really is interested in the welfare and overall satisfaction of those who work here."

In addition, the managers and officers in this sample appeared to be out of touch with the needs and desires of lower level employees. It is ironic to note that nonexempts rated quality circles the least favorably, for example, despite the fact that they are the main target of employee involvement programs. Similarly, nonexempt employees were least accepting of job posting, a main vehicle in the personnel system to help lower employees advance up the ladder. It is possible that these results stem from the fact that the system lacked credibility, as many employees believed management was simply going through the motions of posting a job opening. Nearly half of the respondents (44%), for example, agreed with the empathic item, "Often jobs are posted that are already filled."

The low rating of flextime by nonexempt employees, a rather surprising result, may be due to the restriction placed on the use of this program by lower level workers. As noted previously, one division had altered the official flextime system for clerical workers and made them sign a work schedule identifying the days they were going to flex in advance. Whereas the company officially had a flextime program that was open to all employees, local managers had placed unofficial restrictions on nonexempt workers' use of flextime.

The less favorable rating of flextime by officers and managers may be due to the belief that the innovation has resulted in lower productivity. For example, when approving the questionnaire for distribution, the top line manager of the marketing unit made a single revision by adding the item, "Flextime has hurt the service level provided by my unit." It may also be that flextime had little impact on officers' and managers' daily working environment, which supports the findings of a recent study showing that flextime had the least impact on high level employees.[2]

As an increasing number of human resource programs with superficial impact are adopted, over time, employee cynicism develops. "What basic deficiency is this program attempting to mask *this* time?" Employees are led to question the formal rationale given by executives to support the introduction of a new program and develop informal ones. For example, only 19% of the respondents disagreed with the statement, "Flexible benefits is designed to make VIC money." Ironically, the adopters of this program truly felt it was a magnanimous step forward in the direction of giving employees greater choice in the design of their benefits package.

Applying the Halo Effect to HRM Innovation

A second explanation for the positive attitudes senior employees hold toward HRM innovation is because they have a *halo effect* regarding their overall attitudes toward work.[3] Because officers and managers have achieved a relatively high stature in their jobs, they tend to rate all aspects of the workplace, including new personnel programs, more favorably than other employees. Higher level employees' greater decision-making authority, better pay, status afforded by their positions, and other conditions related to their jobs may foster a general enthusiasm about HRM innovations.

Certainly, the significant differences in employee responses by salary grade group to the items on the overall work environment scale support this notion (SNK$_{.05}$, 1625 df, critical value .10). Officers and managers were the most

Table 7.1
Partial Correlation between Acceptance of Innovation and Salary Grade Holding Work Environment Constant and Acceptance of Innovation and Work Environment Holding Salary Grade Constant

Innovation	Partial Correlation of Acceptance and Work Environment Holding Salary Constant	Significance	Partial Correlation of Acceptance and Salary Holding Work Environment Constant	Significance
Flextime	.06	P < .0001	.0006	P < .28
Job Posting	.16	P < .0001	.004	P < .007
Cash Award	.13	P < .0001	.003	P < .02
Fitness Program	.08	P < .0001	.009	P < .0001
Flexible Benefits	.03	P < .0001	.006	P < .0008
Quality Circles	.08	P < .0001	.003	P < .01
Newsletter	.08	P < .0001	.03	P < .001
Peer Award	.22	P < .0001	.003	P < .27

favorable with a mean acceptance of 2.38. Professionals came next with a mean of 2.69, and nonexempt employees were ranked last with 2.80. Thus if senior employees have the tendency to rate their working environments favorably, perhaps they also have the propensity to be accepting of any new work behavior.

Support for the halo effect is provided by the results of the partial correlation analysis shown in Table 7.1. In all cases, the partial correlations of acceptance of innovation and attitudes toward the work environment holding salary grade constant are higher than the partial correlations of acceptance of innovation and salary grade holding work environment constant.

Approval Rights and Acceptance

A third main explanation for the hierarchical differences is that senior employees or a member of their group *participated* in the decision to adopt the programs. Many scholars such as V. Vroom and A. G. Jago have observed that participation in decision making can improve the acceptance of the decision.[4] Similarly, Ed Lawler found that performance-based compensation systems were the most effective when employees participated in their design.[5] He noted four reasons for the greater effectiveness of programs designed using participation: employees have more information about the system, they are committed to it, they have control over it, and they trust the program. For all of these reasons, officers and managers may have greater acceptance of human resource innovations than lower employees.

In large organizations, however, it is unlikely that all officers and managers participated in decisions regarding the adoption of a HRM innovation. Even if some upper managers did not directly participate in program decision making, perhaps they have greater acceptance simply because their managerial role affords them the *opportunity* to have approval rights or input. Higher level employees' possession of the decision making authority to approve or influence the adoption of new HRM programs may facilitate acceptance for an additional reason. Perhaps some senior managers and executive groups engage in a quid pro quo game of politics. An executive may support one program currently touted by a colleague in exchange for support for a future program that the executive may introduce.

Regardless of the overarching explanation for these differences by levels, the hierarchical results raise a fundamental issue related to decision making regarding the design and adoption of HRM programs. Rarely are lower level employees systematically consulted before the adoption of new programs, such as quality circles. If more employees from lower and middle levels were involved, perhaps the end result would better reflect their interests.

Personality and Acceptance

An alternative explanation to those regarding hierarchical level is that some employees may have the disposition to favorably evaluate human resource innovations and their work environment, in general. Although not nearly as conclusive as the findings supporting the positive relationship between hierarchical level and acceptance of personnel innovation, the results also provide some support for the notion that individual personality differences influence acceptance. The results showing a positive correlation between favorable attitudes toward the work environment and acceptance gives some credence to the renewed argument in the organizational behavior literature to take a dispositional approach to job attitudes, in which the role of the person is emphasized.[6] It may be that if an employee rates his or her organizational climate favorably, he or she may also view new personnel programs favorably.

EQUITY AND ACCEPTANCE OF HRM INNOVATION

The results of the study suggest that acceptance is positively related to the amount of perceived fairness in the relative distribution of the innovation's benefits and costs. Many of the negative empathic items on the survey, which were derived from group and individual interviews, were related to issues of equity in the design or implementation of the innovations. It is useful to recall, for example, that over a third of the respondents (37% and 38%, respectively) agreed with the items, "People who work in lower level jobs are less likely to get a cash award" and "It's not fair that some employees like receptionists (or people who work in the data center) can't flex because they have to cover their work areas." Remember that almost half of the respondents (43%) agreed with the item, "Getting a cash award largely depends on your boss's sales ability."

Many employees commented on equity issues regarding the innovations, and the following employee remarks concerning cash awards are typical. Some employees, for example, were disturbed that outstanding individual achievement awards were sometimes being given to an individual who is contributing to a team effort "as a team leader, doing none of the work, but getting all the awards. Why aren't the people that work overtime getting some of the credit? Reporting statuses don't take too much effort. It is a real farce. No credit is given to people who come in day in and day out and do their job. They are taken for granted." As the remark implies, some positions are more visible and more likely to allow for "perceived outstanding performance" than others.

Other employees were upset when "two out of three on a team have been given cash awards . . . the third was not recognized—unfair practice." Companies may be giving mixed messages to employees. Employees are unsure whether teamwork or individual achievement is what ultimately is being rewarded.

Still other employees are troubled by situations in which they have a manager who is a less capable people manager than his or her peers. As one employee wrote, for example, "The nominating process (for the achievement awards) is not well implemented. My supervisor couldn't care less about his area, so he doesn't push us to submit nominations. Shouldn't he/she be motivated?"

Clearly, an area ripe for future research is the refinement and application of equity theory[7] to models of acceptance of innovation. Who *are* the comparison persons or groups that are evaluated when equity assessments are made? How do equity assessments affect attitudes toward and motivation to use the innovations?

The relevant persons or groups may vary within and between innovations. In the case of the cash award, an individual is likely to evaluate employees with similar jobs in the immediate work area. For Taking Care, employees with less than one year's tenure may compare themselves with employees with more than a year's service who are not restricted from using the fitness center. Thus negative attitudes can be derived from the exclusion from using an innovation. As a Data Processing secretary who has worked for VIC for over eight years commented on the exclusion of part-time workers from use of the fitness center, "You don't really miss something, until you don't have it." As for an example of comparison differences within an innovation, a female clerical worker's assessment of the fairness in the distribution of a cash award might be influenced by whether an outstanding female coworker was the recipient, whereas an officer might be more influenced by whether an officer was on the selection committee.

But as A. Bandura points out, "Verdicts about the worthiness of innovations ultimately rest on value systems. The same distribution of benefits can be viewed favorably or unfavorably, depending on whether it is judged from a utilitarian perspective or an equity perspective."[8] Whether one possesses a predominantly utilitarian or equity perspective regarding the relative benefits of an innovation often depends on one's hierarchical group membership. People at the top of pyramids seldom are concerned about equity, whereas those at the middle and bottom often are very concerned.

IMPACT OF INNOVATION CHARACTERISTICS ON ACCEPTANCE

This study has clearly demonstrated that human resource innovations that improve the quality of life of many organizational members receive high acceptance. Of the eight innovations adopted at VIC, only one significantly improved the quality of life of many organizational members—flextime, the innovation that received the greatest acceptance, 94% of all respondents agreed with the item, "Flextime has helped people better integrate their working day with the demands of their private lives." Seventy-nine percent of the respondents agreed with the statement, "Flextime is very important to me." In contrast, only 4% agreed with the item, "The Flexible Spending Account is very important to me," and only 5% of Financial Services respondents rated People Are Tops as being important to them.

Similarly, 91% of the respondents agreed with the statement, "Overall, flextime is a great program and should be continued." Only 17% agreed that cash awards should be continued. Only 10% wanted to see flexible benefits continued. Clearly, flextime was the innovation that mattered most to employees.

Flextime also may have received high acceptance, because it was more integral to the daily working environment than the other innovations. Like a car, there are some parts that are standard and the car cannot operate without, and there are others that are optional and have little impact on the way the vehicle runs.

Unlike flextime, employees viewed innovations such as quality circles as peripheral to the work of the organization. For example, as one employee wrote, "Innovation Through Involvement is a farce and doesn't tackle real problems.

It strikes me as a make work project.'' Still another employee commented, ''The quality circle in our area took 43 meetings to come up with an innocuous, extremely general ''problem'' (which most noncircle members did not feel was a problem at all). What a waste of time!''

In a recent review, T. Cummings and S. Mohrman distinguish between process and maintenance organizational innovations,[9] a distinction that can aptly be applied to flextime and quality circles, which both involve the HRM policy area of employee influence. Once an organization adopts flextime, little maintenance or redesign work is needed to make the innovation operate smoothly. The nature and scope of employee participation in decision making is well defined and easily integrated into the existing authority structure.

In contrast, in order to ensure the long-term effectiveness of a quality circle program, constant attention and fine tuning are needed and the perimeters defining the limits of employee participation in decision making are often unclear. It is unlikely that quality circles could be effective over the long run, unless their introduction is done in sync with some additional concomitant changes that affect the organization's authority structure (e.g., profit-sharing, information-sharing). Indeed, research has shown that quality circles have often failed because they *didn't* significantly change an organization's authority structure.[10] Over the long term, integration into organizational systems is required for institutionalization.[11] Undoubtedly, future research is needed to identify the specific properties of innovations that make them an integral part of the working environment and beneficial to the quality of work life of members. The results from the panel of experts' ratings of frequency, empowerment, intensity, and performance impact were inconclusive, largely because of small sample size. However, this study's work on the impact of the dimensions of innovations on acceptance is useful, if only in terms of its encouragement to scholars to start thinking about human resource management innovations as having social properties that can be compared.

HRM Integration

Overall, the integration of many human resource innovations into the daily working environment is limited. Most human resource innovations are viewed as *programs*, which are often extraneous to daily work activities and consequently, the extent to which they change the organization's social system is generally minor or short-lived. Because of this, when other work priorities come along, support for human resource practices quickly wanes. For example, the reorganization of the marketing group had a negative impact on the *Grapevine* and the People Are Tops program. Senior management decided to reinstate the *Grapevine* and ''reintroduce PAT'' only after the dust began to settle. Perhaps the more that employees perceive an innovation not as a separate program, but rather as part of the daily working environment, the greater the chances for its long-term acceptance.

Certainly, the American experience with quality circles provides an appropriate example. In his book, *High-Involvement Management*, Ed Lawler reviews the history of quality circles in the United States and concludes:

they are usually not a viable long-term participative strategy for organizations in the United States. . . . As long as they are viewed as programs (which they are in most organizations), they are inevitably subject to elimination or curtailment. . . . the widespread adoption of quality circles may tell us something about how American management thinks about organizational change and participation . . . the two features that make them so attractive . . . is their programmic nature and the fact that they *do not* change the organization. . . . they do not move power away from the traditional hierarchy.[12]

As Lawler's statement suggests, there is a clear relationship between human resource innovation and organizational change. New work practices that are viewed as programs will probably have little long-term influence on an organization's social system. Employees will perceive these programs as superficial attempts to manipulate the work environment.

FUTURE RESEARCH

This study will hopefully encourage additional research that investigates how to shape HRM innovations to better reflect and meet the interests of employees. The main finding showing that higher level employees accept HRM innovations more than lower level employees, particularly those that are designed for non-managers, needs to be replicated in a variety of firms. The explanations offered for this finding, which include senior employees receive the greatest intangible benefits from HRM innovation, have a halo effect in their attitudes toward work, and either participated in the adoption decision-making process or supported the innovation because of perceived approval rights all provide fertile ground for further empirical work.

An alternative explanation is that executives perceive HR programs to be more effective than lower level employees because of role differences. As noted earlier, senior employees make or influence policy decisions regarding HR programs; employees simply use the programs. Perhaps executives generally overstate program effectiveness because of their role in promulgating organizational effectiveness and promoting the firm's reputation.

Whereas the current research's examination of employee reactions to multiple HRM programs across hierarchical levels and collection of data on actual program use represent a useful beginning, there are a number of additional areas ripe for further study. Future research needs to be done on constituent differences in acceptance of a wide diversity of HRM programs adopted in a large sample of U.S. firms. Whereas the acceptance of innovation scale developed for this study offers a new instrument to measure acceptance of HRM programs, more work should be done to refine the scale and to determine whether there are any identifiable subcomponents of acceptance that are generalizable across innovations. Scholars should also identify the important differences and similarities in the acceptance of technical versus organizational innovations. The preliminary measures of the dimensions of human resource innovations explored with the panel of experts also need to be further refined and validated.

Longitudinal research is needed to improve upon the study's cross-sectional design, particularly when viewed in light of the fact that acceptance of innovation will vary over both a typical organization's life-span and program life-cycle. Although statistical analysis found that innovation age was not correlated with acceptance, it is clear that longitudinal work is desirable. We need to develop process models presenting a life-cycle of acceptance to human resource innovation. As acceptance of many innovations waxes and wanes over time, there may be an optimal level of acceptance. Too early in the innovation's life, too few employees may be aware of the innovation. However, as more employees become aware of it, the novelty of the innovation may have faded and innovators may have begun pulling back on organizational support as they start searching for the next new quick fix to adopt.

In addition, we need to study the impact of the line management and Human Resources department relationship on acceptance, particularly in human resource innovation-resisting organizations. The influence of corporate and local politics on successful implementation should be further examined. Another area for future study is the development and application of a theory of the symbolic role of human resource innovation.

Future study should also compare attitudes between different types of program users for a single innovation. In this way, the program experience variable need not be dichotomous, but a hierarchy of experience could be developed. In this way, a user variable could better acknowledge *levels* of usage of a program. For example, a quality circle participant has a higher user level than someone who just reads the circle newsletter on a regular basis. Also, more study is needed exploring the attitudes of employees excluded from using innovations by design. Nonusers are often overlooked during evaluation, but may have an important influence on long-term program viability, such as in the case of middle managers attitudes toward quality circles.

Because employees fail to use human resource innovations for a variety of reasons ranging from lack of knowledge of them (e.g., cash awards), to a negative assessment of what they have to offer (e.g., flexible benefits), to negative social consequences stemming from using them (e.g., quality circles), it also might be fruitful to investigate employee reaction to *bad* innovations and the *costs* of accepting human resource innovations. For example, one of the costs of using the Flexible Spending Account was that if you didn't use the money you set aside, you lost it. The costs of joining a quality circle or the *Grapevine* might be less time to complete your job requirements, since VIC didn't pay formally for participating in these innovations. AIDS education and testing, drug testing, and no-smoking policies are current examples of innovations whose costs and acceptance may differ widely for organizational members.

As for practical implications, the study suggests that personnel managers should be more market-oriented in their design of new programs. In particular, greater efforts should be made to tap into the attitudes that lower and middle level employees hold toward personnel programs, and to use these findings to tailor new programs. Development of meaningful avenues that allow for greater employee participation in the design and implementation of new programs may be beneficial for their long-term acceptance. The results should also encourage HRM managers to give as much attention to *evaluating* the effectiveness of new programs after their adoption as they typically give to designing them.

Whereas the suggestion to study the effects of participation on the acceptance of human resource innovation may not be viewed as terribly new, it is something that surprisingly all too few managers use in the introduction and implementation of new personnel programs. As one senior line manager in Financial Services adeptly stated:

You've got to have programs where the timing is right for the people. Unless people buy into them and feel its something they need and want and have ownership, after the initial splash, most programs die. Different departments within a company need a different approach. I have a problem with the Human Resources Department. It begins to take on a life of its own—because it functions for its own purpose. There's a lot of red tape. No one wants a separate personnel department, because they don't want someone telling them what to do. Human Resources cannot operate outside the spectrum of the line business, when it comes from outside of functional management, it intrudes.

An important issue raised by this quotation is whether line management would do anything if the Human Resource executives weren't pushing the innovations. Perhaps these comments on the dysfunctional relationship between Human Resources and the rest of the firm and on the lack of integration of many personnel programs into the work of the organization have the most significant implications for future research on human resource innovation.

NOTES

1. L. Smircich, and C. Stubbart, "Management in an Enacted World," *Academy of Management Review* no 10, vol 7: 4 (1981): 724–736.

2. V. K. Narayanan, and R. Nath, "A Field Test of Some Attitudinal and Behavioral Consequences of Flextime," *Journal of Applied Psychology* no. 2 (1982), 214–218.

3. A. Inkeles, and D. Smith, *Becoming Modern: Individual Change in Six Developing Countries* (Cambridge, Mass.: Harvard University Press, 1974).

4. V. Vroom, and A. G. Jago, "On the Validity of the Vroom-Yetton Model," *Journal of Applied Psychology* 63 (1978), 151–162.

5. E. E. Lawler, *Pay and Organizational Development* (Reading, Mass.: Addison-Wesley, 1981).

6. B. M. Staw, N. E. Bell, and J. A. Clausen, "The Dispositional Approach to Job Attitudes: A Lifetime Longitudinal Test," *Administrative Science Quarterly* 31 (1986), 56–77.

7. T. Stacy Adams, "Inequity in Social Exchange," in *Advances in Experimental Social Psychology*, vol. 2 (N.Y.: Academic Press, 1965): 267–299.

8. A. Bandura, *Social Foundations of Thought and Action* (Englewood Cliffs, N.J.: Prentice Hall, 1986), 156.

9. T. Cummings, and S. Mohrman, "Self-Designing Organizations: Towards Implementing Quality-of-Work-Life Innovations," *Research in Organizational Change and Development* 1 (1985), 275–310.

10. E. E. Lawler, *High-Involvement Management* (San Francisco: Jossey-Bass, 1986), 64.

11. J. Cutcher-Gershenfeld, "The Collective Governance of Industrial Relations," doctoral dissertation, MIT (1987).

12. Lawler, "High-Involvement Management," 64.

Appendix: Human Resource Programs Questionnaire

APPENDIX: HUMAN RESOURCE PROGRAMS QUESTIONNAIRE - (Department Name)

SECTION ONE - FLEXTIME

Listed below are some statements about flextime. You are to indicate your own personal feelings about flextime by marking how much you agree with the statements. Write a number in each blank using this scale:

1	2	3	4	5
Strongly Agree	Agree	Neither Agree nor Disagree	Disagree	Strongly Disagree

_____ 1. Flextime has helped people better integrate their working day with the demands of their private lives.

_____ 2. I am familiar with the main features of flextime.*

_____ 3. Flextime is very important me.*

_____ 4. I wish there were a different way of keeping track of my hours than signing the time sheets. (R)

_____ 5. Flextime affects my performance on the job.

_____ 6. Flextime has helped improve my productivity.

_____ 7. It's good we have an hour lunch period, because almost everyone needs an hour for lunch.

_____ 8. A lot of people abuse flextime in my area. (R)

_____ 9. Overall, I think flextime is very well run.*

_____ 10. My transportation to and from work has been improved by flextime.

_____ 11. Flextime has helped improve my morale.

_____ 12. In general, I like the way flextime is designed.*

_____ 13. It's not fair that some employees like (receptionists) can't flex early on certain days because they have to cover their work area. (R)

_____ 14. My immediate supervisor supports flextime.*

_____ 15. In general, communication on flextime has been good.*

_____ 16. Overall, flextime is a great program and should be continued.*

_____ 17. Flextime has little importance to me.* (R)

_____ 18. Employees should have more flexibility in deciding their core hours.

_____ 19. It wouldn't bother me if flextime were discontinued.* (R)

_____ 20. A lot of improvement should be made in the way flextime is run.* (R)

_____ 21. Flextime has hurt the service level provided by my unit. (R)(FS only)

SECTION TWO - JOB OPPORTUNITIES PROGRAM

Listed below are some statements about the Job Opportunities Program (JOP). You are to indicate your own personal feelings about JOP by marking how much you agree with the statements. Write a number in each blank using this scale:

1	2	3	4	5
Strongly Agree	Agree	Neither Agree nor Disagree	Disagree	Strongly Disagree

_____ 1. The Job Opportunities Program has encouraged employee initiative in the choice and direction of careers.

_____ 2. Often jobs are posted that are already filled. (R)

_____ 3. JOP has given employees the opportunity to improve their own work situation.

_____ 4. It would be good if officer jobs were posted.

_____ 5. In general, this program is unfair. (R)

_____ 6. The job posting procedure is too bureaucratic. (R)

_____ 7. It's nice to know job posting is there.

_____ 8. Overall, JOP is a great program and should be continued.*

_____ 9. A lot of improvement should be made in the way job posting is run.* (R)

_____ 10. The Job Opportunities Program affects my performance on the job.

_____ 11. My immediate supervisor supports the Job Opportunities Program.*

_____ 12. Job posting has decreased turnover.

_____ 13. Overall, I think the Job Opportunities Program is very well run.*

_____ 14. Job posting has helped achieve our affirmative action goals.

_____ 15. This program effectively publicizes internal job opportunities.

_____ 16. I am familiar with the main features of the job Opportunities Program.*

_____ 17. The Job Opportunities Program has little importance to me.* (R)

_____ 18. It wouldn't bother me if job posting were discontinued.* (R)

_____ 19. In general, I like the way the Job Opportunities Program is designed.*

_____ 20. The Job Opportunities Program is very important to me.*

_____ 21. In general, communication on JOP has been good.*

_____ 22a. I wish we still had separate posting for FSD jobs. (FS only)

_____ 22b. It would be good if job announcements were available via a CRT. (DP only)

SECTION THREE - THE OUTSTANDING ACHIEVEMENT AWARD PROGRAM

Listed below are some statements about The Outstanding Achievement Awards (TOAAP). you are to indicate your own personal feelings about TOAAP by marking how much you agree with the statements. Write a number in each blank using this scale:

1	2	3	4	5
Strongly Agree	Agree	Neither Agree nor Disagree	Disagree	Strongly Disagree

_____ 1. I am familiar with the main features of TOAAP.*

_____ 2. TOAAP pays cash bonuses for employees' outstanding one time achievements.

_____ 3. TOAAP is very important to me.*

_____ 4. Overall, I think TOAAP is very well run.*

_____ 5. In general, communication on TOAAP has been good.*

_____ 6. Deserving employees have received this award.

_____ 7. Getting a TOAAP largely depends on your boss's sales ability.

_____ 8. A lot of improvement should be made in the way TOAAP is run.* (R)

_____ 9. TOAAP should recognize group achievements as well as individual ones.

_____ 10.   It wouldn't bother me if TOAAP were discontinued.* (R)

_____ 11.   In general, I like the way TOAAP is designed.*

_____ 12.   It's good that my division VP must sign off on my unit's nominations.

_____ 13.   TOAAP affects my performance on the job.

_____ 14.   Overall, TOAAP is a great program and should be continued.*

_____ 15.   I'd like to know more about who won the award and what they did.

_____ 16.   It would be good if the amount of bonus received were publicized.

_____ 17.   This program has made me more motivated in my work.

_____ 18.   My immediate supervisor supports TOAAP.*

_____ 19.   TOAAP helps create a team atmosphere.

_____ 20.   People who work in lower level jobs are less likely to get a TOAAP.(R)

_____ 21.   TOAAP has little importance to me.* (R)

_____ 22.   My manager won't nominate me for a TOAAP even if I deserve it. (R)

_____ 23.   If I receive a TOAAP, I would like it to be publicized.

SECTION FOUR - TAKING CARE

Listed below are some statements about Taking Care. You are to indicate your own personal feelings bout Taking Care by marking how much you agree with the statements. Write a number in each blank using this scale:

1	2	3	4	5
Strongly Agree	Agree	Neither Agree nor Disagree	Disagree	Strongly Disagree

_____ 1.   I am familiar with the main features of Taking Care.*

_____ 2.   Taking Care has saved the Company money by lowering health care costs.

_____ 3.   Taking Care has helped improve the fitness of employees.

_____ 4.   In general, communication on Taking Care has been good.*

_____ 5.   The managing of signing up to use the fitness center has been well done.

_____ 6. I like to receive the Taking Care newsletter.

_____ 7. Taking Care is connected with the recent increase in our deductible level for group coverage of medical benefits.

_____ 8. The Patient Advocate Program is part of the Taking Care program.

_____ 9. People who want to use the fitness center should pay for their own physical.

_____ 10. The fitness center is the best feature of Taking Care.

_____ 11. This program is a waste of Company money. (R)

_____ 12. Taking Care is very important to me.*

_____ 13. Overall, Taking Care is a great program and should be continued.*

_____ 14. Taking Care affects my performance on the job.

_____ 15. A lot of improvement should be made in the way Taking Care is run.* (R)

_____ 16. Taking Care has reinforced positive lifestyle & medical self-care.

_____ 17. Taking Care has little importance to me.* (R)

_____ 18. Overall, I think Taking Care is very well run.*

_____ 19. My immediate supervisor supports Taking Care.*

_____ 20. In general, I like the way Taking Care is designed.*

_____ 21. It wouldn't bother me if Taking Care were discontinued.* (R)

SECTION FIVE - FLEXIBLE SPENDING ACCOUNT

Listed below are some statements about The Flexible Spending Account (FSA). You are to indicate your own personal feelings about FSA by marking how much you agree with the statements. Write a number in each blank using this scale:

1	2	3	4	5
Strongly Agree	Agree	Neither Agree nor Disagree	Disagree	Strongly Disagree

_____ 1. The Flexible Spending Account has little importance to me.* (R)

_____ 2. In general, communication on FSA has been good.*

_____ 3. The "use it or lose it" rule discourages me from signing up for FSA. (R)

_____ 4. I am familiar with the main features of The Flexible Spending Account.*

_____ 5. This program is designed to make VIC money. (R)

_____ 6. It's too difficult to predict your health expenses not covered by the regular policy a year in advance. (R)

_____ 7. This program is good for employees with child care needs.

_____ 8. It wouldn't bother me if FSA were discontinued..* (R)

_____ 9. FSA helps employees pay for certain health and dependent-care expenses with salary that isn't taxable.

_____ 10. It would be good if there were day care facilities at work.

_____ 11. FSA affects my performance on the job.

_____ 12. My immediate supervisor supports FSA.*

_____ 13. Overall, I think the Flexible Spending Account is very well run.*

_____ 14. Overall, FSA is a great program and should be continued.*

_____ 15. In general, I like the way FSA is designed.*

_____ 16. I've heard it takes people too long to get their FSA check. (R)

_____ 17. VIC's FSA administrative requirements are more stringent than the law requires. (R)

_____ 18. FSA is very important to me.*

_____ 19. A lot of improvement should be made in the way FSA is run.* (R)

SECTION SIX - INNOVATION THROUGH INVOLVEMENT

Listed below are some statements about Innovation Through Involvement (ITI). You are to indicate your own personal feelings about ITI by marking how much you agree with the statements. Write a number in each blank using this scale:

1	2	3	4	5
Strongly Agree	Agree	Neither Agree nor Disagree	Disagree	Strongly Disagree

_____ 1. ITI lets people learn skills they usually wouldn't learn on the job.

_____ 2. In general, ITI is a great program and should be continued.*

_____ 3. ITI should be able to solve problems involving more than one work area.

_____ 4. A lot of improvement should be made in the way ITI is run.* (R)

_____ 5. In general, management has followed through on each ITI recommendation.

_____ 6. ITI groups tend to tackle only the solvable problems. (R)

_____ 7. It would be good if more officers and managers participated in ITI.

_____ 8. ITI is a program mainly for jobs involving processing insurance forms.

_____ 9. Participation in ITI is voluntary.

_____ 10. People who participate in ITI receive enough recognition.

_____ 11. In general, I like the way ITI is designed.

_____ 12. At first, ITI got a lot of hype, but now you don't hear much about it. (R)

_____ 13. Overall, ITI has helped make employees more involved in their jobs.

_____ 14. My immediate supervisor supports ITI.*

_____ 15. ITI is very important to me.*

_____ 16. It wouldn't bother me if ITI were discontinued.* (R)

_____ 17. ITI affects my performance on the job.

_____ 18. I am familiar with the main features of ITI.*

_____ 19. ITI has little importance to me.* (R)

_____ 20. ITI has improved communication in my area.

_____ 21. In general, I think ITI is very well run.*

_____ 22. ITI has fostered teamwork.*

_____ 23. The ITI problem-solving cycle takes too long. (R)

_____ 24. In general, communication on ITI has been good.*

SECTION SEVEN - THE PEOPLE ARE TOPS RECOGNITION PROGRAM (FS only)

Listed below are some statements about The People Are Tops Recognition Program
(PAT). You are to indicate your own personal feelings about PAT by marking how
much you agree with the statements. Write a number in each blank using this
scale:

1	2	3	4	5
Strongly Agree	Agree	Neither Agree nor Disagree	Disagree	Strongly Disagree

_____ 1.   Deserving employees receive this award.

_____ 2.   The PAT program rewards quality work and outstanding personal
            service.

_____ 3.   In general, communication on the PAT program has been good.*

_____ 4.   It wouldn't bother me if PAT were discontinued.* (R)

_____ 5.   My immediate supervisor supports the PAT program.*

_____ 6.   Sometimes people who receive a PAT award are embarrassed. (R)

_____ 7.   In general, the PAT award is a great program and should be
            continued.*

_____ 8.   There is too much paperwork involved in nominating someone. (R)

_____ 9.   The PAT program motivates employees to apply their best effort.

_____ 10.   Overall, I think the PAT program is very well run.*

_____ 11.   I am familiar with the main features of the PAT program.*

_____ 12.   The fun and games that can go with announcing the PAT award
            sometimes takes away from its sincerity. (R)

_____ 13.   More supervisors should receive PAT awards.

_____ 14.   The Perfect Attendance Award (PAA) emphasizes the importance of
            attendance to all non-officers.

_____ 15.   I understand the difference between a PAT award and a SPOT award.

_____ 16.   The PAT program has little importance to me.* (R)

_____ 17.   The PAT award provides positive reinforcement from your peers.

_____ 18.   The PAT program affects my performance on the job.

_____ 19.   Overall, I like the way the PAT program is designed.*

_____ 20.   The PAT program is very important to me.*

_____ 21.   A lot of improvement should be made in the way PAT is run. (R)

_____ 22.   The PAT program is designed for non-officer people.

SECTION EIGHT - THE GRAPEVINE (FS only)

Listed below are some statements about the <u>Grapevine</u>. You are to indicate your own personal feelings about the <u>Grapevine</u> by marking how much you agree with the statements. Write a number in each blank using this scale:

1	2	3	4	5
Strongly Agree	Agree	Neither Agree nor Disagree	Disagree	Strongly Disagree

_____ 1.   The <u>Grapevine</u> has helped me keep better informed.

_____ 2.   The <u>Grapevine</u> is very important to me.*

_____ 3.   The <u>Grapevine</u> has helped create a positive image of FSD.

_____ 4.   In general, communication on the <u>Grapevine</u> has been good.*

_____ 5.   The <u>Grapevine</u> helps recognize people's achievements.

_____ 6.   My immediate supervisor supports the <u>Grapevine</u>.*

_____ 7.   Anyone can volunteer to participate on the <u>Grapevine</u> staff.

_____ 8.   I am familiar with the main features of the <u>Grapevine</u>.*

_____ 9.   The <u>Grapevine</u> is uncensored by management.

_____ 10.   Overall, I like the way the <u>Grapevine</u> is designed.*

_____ 11.   The <u>Grapevine</u> is a lot more interesting to read than other company publications.

_____ 12.   Overall, I think the <u>Grapevine</u> is very well run.*

_____ 13.   The <u>Grapevine</u> positively affects my performance on the job.

_____ 14.   Overall, the <u>Grapevine</u> is a great program and should be continued.*

_____ 15.   In general, the <u>Grapevine</u> makes me feel good about being an employee in the Financial Services Department.

_____ 16.   It does a good job at using humor to poke fun at work problems.

_____ 17.   The <u>Grapevine</u> has little importance to me.* (R)

_____ 18.   It helps make me feel closer to the Senior VP and his staff.

_____ 19.   I find the <u>Grapevine</u> very entertaining.

_____ 20.   A lot of improvement should be made in the way the <u>Grapevine</u> is run.* (R)

_____ 21.   The <u>Grapevine</u> lets employees communicate issues to top management.

_____ 22.   It wouldn't bother me if the <u>Grapevine</u> were discontinued.*

SECTION NINE - WORK ENVIRONMENT

Listed below are some statements about the work environment. You are to indicate your own personal feelings about the work environment by marking how much you agree with the statements. Write a number in each blank using this scale:

1	2	3	4	5
Strongly Agree	Agree	Neither Agree nor Disagree	Disagree	Strongly Disagree

_____ 1.   (DP or Marketing Group) Human Resources does a good job of carrying out programs.

_____ 2.   (FS and DP) top management really is interested in the welfare and overall satisfaction of those who work here.

_____ 3.   My immediate supervisor places a high priority on my personal work needs.

_____ 4.   Filling out this survey is a good way to let management know how I feel about these programs.

_____ 5.   My supervisor usually backs new human resource programs.

_____ 6.   The HR department does a good job of administering programs.

_____ 7.   (FS and DP) top management is generally respected by employees.

_____ 8.   Overall, people are open to trying new ways of managing.

_____ 9.   I respect the people who work in (DP and Marketing Group) Human Resources.

_____ 10.   In general, VIC is a company that cares about its employees.

_____ 11.   (Top executive name) really cares about employee welfare.

_____ 12. I often doubt the truth of what my supervisor tells us. (R)

_____ 13. The longer you work for (FS and DP), the more you feel you belong.

_____ 14. The head of (FS and DP) is very concerned about the needs of employees.

_____ 15. VIC shows very little interest in developing employees for better jobs. (R)

_____ 16. VIC's benefits programs fit my needs.

_____ 17. A lot of personnel programs just come and go around here. (R)

_____ 18. In general, my supervisor is open to progressive people practices.

_____ 19. There are adequate opportunities for employees to learn about available job openings.

_____ 20. My supervisor is concerned about helping his people get ahead.

_____ 21. Most personnel programs that are tried in my division are successful.

_____ 22. People in my division trust each other.

_____ 23. I am proud to tell people I work for the (FS or DP) Department.

_____ 24. I am often bothered by too much pressure on the job.

_____ 25. From what I know, (FS or DP) identifies and recognizes people who work the hardest and contribute the most.

_____ 26. I can disagree with my supervisor without fear of reprisal.

_____ 27. I feel encouraged to come up with new and better ways of doing things.

_____ 28. My supervisor does a good job of building teamwork.

_____ 29. From what I know, personnel policies are uniformly administered from division to division.

_____ 30. My supervisor recognizes and appreciates good work and tells us so.

_____ 31. Sufficient effort is made to get the opinions and thinking of people who work here.

_____ 32. (FS or DP) management will carefully consider problems brought to its attention by this survey.

_____ 33. In general, communications in my unit are good.

_____ 34. The decisions management makes in my department are usually fair.

_____ 35. Most of the time its safe to say what you think around here.

_____ 36. I respect my immediate supervisor.

_____ 37. In general, the reporting structure in my area will remain constant in the future.

_____ 38. The biggest personnel problem in (FS or DP) is poor communications. (R)

_____ 39. There's too great an emphasis on controlling costs around here. (R)

_____ 40. I wish I had more opportunity to make suggestions to improve my work. (R)

_____ 41. People are recognized in my unit for doing superior work.

_____ 42. My supervisor watches over my shoulder too much. (R)

_____ 43. People who work in (FS) are the most productive VIC employees.

_____ 44. The AMG reorganization has generally had a negative impact on my feelings toward many of the programs in this survey. (FS only)

SECTION TEN - BACKGROUND

The following questions ask information about your involvement in these programs and your background. None of your individual responses on any of these items will be made available to corporate personnel. Check all that apply.

A. Program Use

    1. TOAAP   2. ITI

        _____ Received award   _____ Circle member
        _____ Nominated someone   _____ Facilitator
        _____ Never received award   _____ Leader
              or nominated anyone   _____ Don't
        _____ I'm on an incentive plan,   participate in ITI
              & am ineligible.   _____ Steering
        _____ If TOAAP winners posted   Committee/Admin.
              on the bulletin board, I'd   _____ Read ITI
              read the announcement.   Newsletter
                                                          _____ Am not in circle,
                                                                but would like to
                                                                join one

3. Flextime

_____ Can usually work noncore hours

_____ I have work restrictions on
my choice of hours

4. Taking Care

_____ Usually don't
read newsletter

_____ Signed up for
Fitness Center
_____ Watched video
_____ Participated in
support activity
(e.g., weight
loss contest)

5. Job Opportunities

_____ Never posted
_____ Posted for job
_____ Hired-job poster

B. BIOGRAPHICAL

(FS Divisions listed as examples)

1. Division

_____ A&CS _____ Marketing
_____ Other_____ /Actuarial
_____ Underwriting

2. Sex

_____ Male
_____ Female

3. Race

_____ White _____ Black
_____ Hispanic _____ American Indian/or
_____ Asian or   Alaskan Native
       Pacific Is.

4. Salary Grade

_____ S.G. 26-35
_____ S.G. 36-46
_____ S.G. 47 and
       above

5. I am eligible for overtime _____ (Yes or No)

6. Years with Company _____ Less than one year
                       _____ 1-5 years
                       _____ 6-10 years
                       _____ 11-15 years
                       _____ 16 years or more

COMMENTS

List the human resource issues or programs that you feel need to be improved
(if any) and why:

_____

_____

_____

_____

_____

_____

Write any additional comments you'd like to make on this page:

* = Comparable items; (R) = Reverse scoring

FS = Financial Services
DP = Data Processing

Index

About the Author

ELLEN ERNST KOSSEK is Assistant Professor of Human Resource Management at the School of Labor and Industrial Relations at Michigan State University. Kossek has worked on human resource issues for IBM, GTE, Hitachi, and Deere and Company in the United States, Europe, and Japan.